MORALITY FOR MODERNS

VIBS

Volume 36

MORALITY FOR MODERNS

Corbin Fowler

Amsterdam - Atlanta, GA 1996

Cover design by Chris Kok based on a photograph, © 1984 by Robert Ginsberg, of statuary by Gustav Vigeland in the Frogner Park, Oslo, Norway.

∞ The paper on which this book is printed meets the requirements of "ISO 9706:1994, Information and documentation - Paper for documents - Requirements for permanence".

ISBN: 90-5183-924-3 (CIP)

Printed in The Netherlands

Dedication

Dedicated to the memory of the liberal and radical idealism of the sixties, and to the love which nurtures my present: Patti and Corbin Sterling.

CONTENTS

FOREWORD

Corbin Fowler approaches the contemporary crisis in morality by appealing to lived experience, common-sense terms, classical insights, and tested values. Sailing the ship of philosophical inquiry between the whirlpool of relativism and the rocks of authoritarianism, Fowler dispels the treacherous mists that beset ethical thought. He makes an elegant, sensible case for balancing our social obligations with self-regarding care. While acknowledging the broad realm of differences that follow from exercise of freedom, Fowler makes a stand for the shared principles that bond us together as a community.

This search for humane answers to the perennial question, "Why should we live morally?", is launched most fittingly by that modern form of dialogue–the cocktail party. In the voyage that ensues, Fowler attends to the integrity of philosophical discourse as well as to the integrity of the moral life.

Robert Ginsberg
Executive Editor

PREFACE

For thousands of years, people have discussed and debated the nature of moral right and wrong. The reflections in this book are my contribution to this debate. Must morality be based upon religious faith or belief in God? Is morality equivalent with following "the rules" and respecting law and order? Is unselfishness merely a naive illusion which fosters neurotic and self-destructive behavior? Are we even capable of acting unselfishly? Is moral truth like beauty, existing only in the eyes of the beholder? Are there universal moral standards, or are moral "facts" always relative to the culture in which you happen to live? Is it in our rational self-interest to live morally, or would we be better off living a life of calculated deception and manipulation, using others only as means to our ends? Are we free agents who are personally responsible for our good and bad deeds, or are we the complex products of our biological, physical, and social environments? These are the issues we will explore.

I began writing this book in 1979, spurred on by several trends of the post-1960s. One of these trends was a turning away from "social consciousness" and activism to a preoccupation with the self. The activism of the 1960s, the long non-victorious war against Vietnam, and the Watergate scandal had severely demoralized the American psyche. Americans longed desperately to feel good about themselves and their nation. In their rush to make themselves feel good, Americans moved in an unhealthy direction, leaping from the frying pan into the fire (though heavily sedated against the pain of this fire). Another trend continued among college youth and segments of the faculty: a widespread disdain of objectivity, accompanied by the belief that all truth and values were culturally relative or the creation of our minds. Being from the 1960s, and being a young college teacher during the 1970s, I was all-too-familiar with this phenomenon. While I understood and had sympathy for this outpouring of relativism, I was convinced that this trend was an unhealthy development. Would the social fabric of morality come unravelled if we wove into it the following convictions?

1. Moral right is determined by individual preferences.
2. Objectivity of values is impossible; it is an illusion.
3. The individual is all-important.

It struck me that in this bag of convictions a crisis was brewing for modern morality.

Twenty-five hundred years ago Plato had written his *Republic* in response to turbulence in his society of Athens. In his city-state the warriors and merchants had brought home news of "civilizations" (barbarians to many Greek minds) whose customs and laws were quite different from theirs. Athens had waged and lost a thirty-year war with Sparta, provoking grave self-doubts among Athenians about whether Athens was god-blessed and whether Athens' ways were the right ways. Prominent intellectuals taught that no absolute values existed and that all truth was relative to individual perspectives. Plato was greatly disturbed by the growing influence of such views. The *Republic* was his literary defense of the existence of value standards which are constant and his defense of the objectivity of moral (and other) knowledge. It represented his intellectual battle with the subjectivity and intellectual anarchy he found rampant in Athens.

As I see it, the *Republic* was not so much a decisive refutation of the opposing schools of thought as it was the construction of a coherent alternative to value subjectivism and relativism. In the late 1970s in America, I felt it imperative to do something similar. With no illusions that my effort could approximate Plato's creativity or genius, I set about to defend morality against various sorts of cultural and intellectual challenges.

Consider the cultural climate of the 1970s. There was a rapid movement away from the social activism which had been inspired by visions of justice for minority groups and women. Throughout the 1960s and early 1970s, visions of a far more humane world had energized large segments of the nation through the Peace Corps, VISTA, hippy flower-power, the civil rights movement, the student movement, the anti-Vietnam War movement, the black power movement, the American Indian movement, etc. Around the world, citizen Davids struggled against institutional Goliaths. The U.S.-U.S.S.R. competition to explore space and U.S. astronauts landing on the moon captured people's imagination and made them believe that anything was possible. Among the young, the conviction flourished that the radically better world they struggled for could be achieved within their lifetimes. The new music, alternative lifestyles, and activism were filled with the joyful conviction that each of us truly is our brothers' (and sisters') keeper.

By the late 1970s such visions and idealistic activism had largely vanished, and many in our society were quite happy to proclaim the demise of the 1960s. The new attitude was that the activism and rebellion of the 1960s had been bad news, an aberration born of the spasms of immature and self-destructive youth. A predominant image of the 1960s activist (like that of the Vietnam veteran) was of an angry and anti-social person, doped-up and burned-out. The profile of the 1960s generation was one of failure, a lost generation which the nation should do its utmost to see was never repeated. Behind their idealistic slogans and banners, these cultural lepers really signified violence, anarchy, and anti-patriotism. No wonder that in the late 1970s the only remnants of 1960s activism were feminism and a struggling environmental movement.

In the place of 1960s values, best-selling books proclaimed a new ethic–the virtues of being selfish and of "looking out for number one." Instead of hippies or yippies, the new ideal was the yuppy who stood for the passionate pursuit of career success and material prosperity... and *within* the Established Order of business and politics. The new message was that the System was the solution. We were urged to immerse ourselves in ourselves. Magazines like *People* were followed by *Us* and *Self*. Would the next magazine be *Me*, which each of us (who could afford to) would promote, and which would feature our own autobiography up to that point, told in a flattering way and containing lots of photos? The political "isms" of the 1960s had been quickly replaced with "Me-ism." The Me-Generation had arrived.

We were on the brink of the Reagan-Bush era of national politics. The Equal Rights Amendment to the Constitution was defeated and conservatives hailed the return to traditional values of family, religion, and patriotism. Americans were fed up with the negative news and trauma they associated with Watergate and the Vietnam war. They were fed up with feeling picked on, humiliated, and impotent at the hands of "fifth-rate countries" like Iran. Americans felt insecure and vulnerable; they longed to feel strong again, to feel good about themselves. Waiting in the wings was Ronald Reagan, who was eager to restore our military might and to emphasize the goodness and God-blessed nature of America in the midst of evil forces in the world. It was not long before Americans would recapture their feeling of Manifest Destiny, the faith that we are a special people of a special country destined by God to greatness in the affairs of nations. Along with the Me-Generation had arrived the Great Communicator.

But why did we feel good about ourselves? Was *this feeling* good... good for us? Alcohol and other drugs can make us feel serene, euphoric, or invincible, but is the pretty illusion of the high worth it? There are many types of addictions, compulsions, and delusions. In no case does the person's feeling good indicate good health or a sound frame of mind. Christopher Lasch[1] was probably right that America is dominated by narcissistic personalities. "Narcissism" here does not just mean a vain, admiration of yourself, but points to severe insecurity and deep ambivalence about your self-worth.[2] Sometimes the narcissist feels as if he or she is utterly charming and God's gift to the world; other times the feeling is of being utterly worthless and unlovable. Narcissists cope with their sense of extreme vulnerability and low self-worth by constantly projecting the appearance of being charming and lovable. They are eager to accept positive and flattering reports about themselves from others and equally ready to reject or downplay any hints that they are uncharming or unlovable. Such negative news feels too threatening to their eggshell sense of self-worth. They are wholly self-absorbed and devote most of their energy to soliciting evidence that they are charming and deflecting evidence to the contrary. They are the P-R (Public Relations) prototype *par excellence.*

Such I feared were the moral red flags of the late 1970s. Unable or unwilling to confront our real problems (personal and societal), Americans were retreating into a reassuring bubble world. Consequently, the highest priority was assigned to personal ambitions (careerism), meditational bliss, New Age elevator music, and maintaining a positive attitude toward oneself. As a teacher, I was often reminded of my students' attraction to "me-ism" and various versions of subjectivism and relativism. There was, for example, the appeal of Richard Bach's best-selling *Illusions,*[3] a book bound to strike a chord with young people's turbulent insecurity and their desire to empower their lives. In that book's tale of "the reluctant messiah" (from the heartland of Indiana), the protagonist maintains that we construct "reality" for ourselves. No limitations apply to us save those which we consciously or unconsciously place upon ourselves. Furthermore, our wills are like magnets so that we attract and are responsible for whatever good or bad that comes our way. But when constructively mobilized, our unlimited will-power is able to transform "reality" however we wish. Indeed, this reluctant messiah confesses that he has found the way to move through earth as if it were water (pure mind over matter).

The irony of the book's title did not escape me. What kind of illusions were being created or played to? This reluctant messiah was just the latest (psychologized) version of one of America's most powerful myths: Superman, Superwoman, Superboy, or Supergirl. Instead of leaping buildings with a single bound, this psychic superman leaps obstacles with a single burst of psychic power. This character's charm lay precisely in his appeal to our infantile fantasies of being at the center of the world and of exercising absolute control. This character was just the latest version of the American mythical hero (usually male) who "pulls himself up by his own bootstraps."

In my view (and also in the traditional view) morality involves learning to recognize limitations, ours and others'. It also involves an abiding commitment to respect other people's needs as coequal with our needs–hence to acknowledge that we are not the center of the world. These I would call the basic conditions of humility, an attitude vital to moral commitment as the world has known it. The cultural climate of the late 1970s was a denial of the need for humility. If 1960s idealism was based largely on fantasies of how rapidly and substantially the world could be improved, if they tended toward destructive results–it was hard to see how the new fantasies of the late 1970s constituted an improvement. Indeed, their potential for causing damage was greater than the 1960s values they were meant to repudiate.

My purpose in writing this book has been to address some of the key theoretical issues of ethics, both for our time and for all times. Two issues I have given emphasis to are the questions of whether morality is best construed as (1) subjective or objective, and (2) as relative or absolute. In Chapter One, I raise these issues through a fictional dialogue. The point there is to draw the tensions between the opposing views as intensely as possible and to introduce some of the key arguments on both sides. The narrator of that story is meant to be portrayed as insightful. Thus, my bias in favor of an objectivist view of morality emerges early in the book. No doubt my bias is also revealed if it appears to the reader that the narrator's intellectual adversary is painted in superficial or drab colors. In the struggle for the readers' hearts and minds, I prefer to think of this as poetic license.

I wrote Chapters Two and Five to make credible the case for the objective and absolute aspects of morality. Chapter Two examines tempting misconceptions about the nature of moral judgments. For example, people often associate morality with the stern authoritarianism of religion, or with the view that elites are entitled to force us to accept their judgment of what we should do or believe. This hierarchical and quasi-fascist view is rightfully repugnant to many of us. Identifying it with morality conceals from us the democratic nature of moral values. As a consequence of this misconception, many people may become so disillusioned with "moralizing" that they would rather pronounce morality hopelessly subjective or relative rather than accept such a harsh model of right and wrong. Their misunderstanding drives them to reject one extreme in favor of another extreme.

Having said a great deal about what morality is *not*, I begin to state my view of what it *is*. In Chapter Three I argue that a key element of moral behavior is unselfish action. I also argue this does not mean we must always sacrifice concern for ourselves in order to protect others' well-being. Distinguishing healthy self-concern from selfish behavior, I argue against the view that says we have no choice but to act selfishly. Moral action, I argue, means striking a balance between thinking too much about yourself and thinking too much about others. Selfish actions are wrong, but so too is self-neglect.

In Chapter Four I present my view of free choice and moral responsibility. These two ideas have played a mighty role in the tradition of Western morality. We would think of morality quite differently, and we would think of people quite differently, if we did not suppose that people usually are morally responsible for their choices. If we thought people never made free choices, we would probably abandon the idea that we are morally responsible beings. Although some thinkers have argued that free will and moral responsibility are only cultural fictions, I defend human free will and responsibility. In this defense, I challenge two suppositions of the traditional attack on free will and moral responsibility. These suppositions are (1) having free will and responsibility depends on our choices *not* being determined, and (2) the overwhelming evidence is that our choices are determined.

Against supposition (1), I argue that our freedom and responsibility are not wed to the falsehood of the doctrine of determinism. Instead, I argue that our freedom and responsibility depend on the kinds of circumstances surrounding our choices, including the kinds of things which cause us to act as we do. This position I call "compatibilism." Against supposition (2), I argue that the evidence for determinism is underwhelming and will remain so. Thus, it is just as reasonable to believe in some form of indeterminism. But if we cannot resolve the question of human free will and responsibility in a straightforward investigation of the truth of determinism, I claim we should turn to other sorts of relevant questions. Would human self-esteem and happiness be gravely damaged if we abandoned the supposition of determinism? Would our self-esteem and happiness be gravely damaged if we abandoned our belief in free will and moral responsibility? The answer to the first question is "no," and the answer to the second is "yes." In conclusion, I argue that *if* our belief in free will and responsibility would be destroyed by believing in the determinism of human choices, we ought to reject such determinism. I call this position "pragmatic compatibilism."

The chapters on egoism and free will are more closely related to the issue of moral subjectivism than you might think. Consider these two assertions: (1) We always act selfishly, (2) Free will and moral responsibility are fictions. If we accept (1) and (2), how much room is left us to consider morality as objective? The answer is "not much." True, objectivist views like utilitarianism would still be possible, but few people are attracted to utilitarianism, and many of us find it distinctly unpalatable.

If so many of us can be so wrong in our thinking that we strongly disagree with both (1) and (2), we should wonder whether we have any grip at all on the true nature of morality! Thus, the views I reject in Chapters Three and Four are a substantial part of the overall attack against viewing moral right and wrong as objective matters of fact. If we were to accept these attacks on unselfishness and free will as simply the most recent results of intellectual progress, we would only contribute to the further balkanization of the moral community... as we each withdraw further into moral subjectivism or relativism. One of my purposes is to offer intellectual resistance to such moral splintering and disenchantment.

In Chapter Five I try to make plausible the existence of an objective common ground for the moral community. I examine various objectivist theories of morality, and I put forward my objectivist theory. I say we ought to do whatever will best promote healthy personal development within the context of justice. My view is eclectic and does not fall neatly into the traditional categories used to classify ethical theories.

My position is that health in general, and healthy self-development in particular, are moral goods. In contrast, sickness and poor self-development are moral evils. Doing what you please when you please is not healthy self-development, but a cancerous growth. Such unrestrained growth is self destructive and other-destructive. Furthermore, justice requires that we all be permitted as much personal growth (to speak broadly) as is compatible with the healthy growth of others. Promoting human happiness and accepting the obligations implied by justice are cornerstones of morality as I see it. Thus, I argue that everyone's self-interest is to encourage justice in society. A society which is dominated by injustice will be a threat to everyone's health and self-development. There must be honor even "among thieves," or the thieves will regret it.

I attempt to refute common objections against the objectivity and absolute nature of some moral standards. Such objections, I argue, are indecisive in each case, and in some instances these subjectivist and relativist objections undermine the objectivity of all values.

I respond to the objection that in no credible way can we conceive of our knowing moral qualities in an objective manner. To this, I propose that such objective knowledge could occur in one of two ways. (1) We can suppose that moral qualities are abstract qualities which really exist in the world, and that we are able to perceive them through the operation of our brain. On this view, the brain is conceived of as more than a computing and storage mechanism, dependent on data about the external world on the delivery systems of our five senses. Instead, the brain is also thought of as a sixth sense-organ, like the eyes, ears, nose, etc. In other words, the brain *perceives* abstract real properties, including moral properties, while the other sense-organs transmit more concrete data to the brain. (2) It could be that moral concepts are objective simply because they are part of the way our species *understands* the experience we gain from our five senses. Following Kant's lead, we could say that just as we categorize our experience in the categorical terms of cause and effect and truth-versus-falsehood, so too we order our experience in terms of moral right versus wrong. On this view, the objectivity of moral judgments means that their truth or falseness is not affected by individual whims or beliefs. But the standard of their truth would not be something *in* the external world. Instead, it would be something about us as human beings: the structure of our conceptual network.

For those who judge a theory's adequacy by how well it fits into current scientific theory, the second of these two theories is bound to seem more credible. It doesn't seem to contradict anything basic to psychology, anthropology or physiology. The first theory, however, does not fit easily into current scientific theory about how we know qualities in the world. Though it is more radical in this respect, it is not beyond the pale of contemporary science. If we are willing to postulate the existence of abstract properties outside of the mind (as Plato and Aristotle[4] did), neurophysiologists and psychologists would only need to hypothesize the existence of corresponding neural mechanisms in our brain which allow us to know such properties. In principle, this is no odder than assuming some brain function which while always receiving "upside-down" visual images of external objects from our eyes' retinas, somehow manages to interpret them as being "rightside-up." If, therefore, science is our contemporary guide to what really exists, I would say that the theory of moral objectivism can be underwritten by science.

In philosophy we speak of a possible doctrine called "solipsism." Variations on its exact meaning occur, but it usually connotes the view that, "So far as I know (with certainty), I am the only conscious thing in existence. Indeed, I might well be the only thing in existence." Let me paraphrase this view as "So far as I know, I am the center of everything." No philosopher I am aware of has viewed solipsism as anything more than a radical skepticism to be ridiculed or refuted.

Psychologists will note how much this doctrine resembles narcissism, an emotional disturbance in which people waiver between euphoria over their supposed extreme charm and the black hole of feeling utterly wretched and unlovable. This book is addressed to a phenomenon related to narcissism: moral solipsism. The moral solipsist is one who believes, or is tempted to believe, that his or her perspective on moral right and wrong is the only perspective which needs to be taken seriously. Such a solipsist may be a narcissist, but typically arrives at this view out of laziness, frustration, or disillusionment. Moral solipsists want to believe morality is objective and shared, but their sad experience and reasoning convinces them that no reliable external standards of right and wrong exist. Thus, they withdraw into the shelter of their own moral perspective.

We are not yet a society of moral solipsists, but we are headed in that direction. Many forces in the world push people to lose their faith in moral community. The movement toward moral solipsism is profoundly unhealthy and to be resisted just as much as the intolerance and cruelty of moral imperialism and religious absolutism. In this book I seek to challenge and undermine the intellectual justifications of moral solipsism. This is necessary if we are to forestall the deconstruction of the moral community. Once we lose faith in the moral common ground, the barbarians who destroy our civilization will be us.

This project began over a decade ago, and I am grateful to many people for their help in preparing the evolving manuscript for publication. For their typing assistance, I thank Helen Molina, Nathalie Moore, Wendy Eidenmuller, Marie Goodenow, Norma Hartmer, Karen Lackovic, Lisa Drake, Carrie James, and especially Diane Harpst. For their review and commentary on selected chapters, I am grateful to my colleagues at Edinboro University: Lucy Bohne, Ed Abegg, and Richard Double. Two people are owed a special thanks. One is Thomas Atwater of Cameron University, who reviewed the entire manuscript and gave both encouragement and helpful critique. The other is my editor, Robert Ginsberg. I thank him for his advice and encouragement, but especially for judging my work to be a worthy contribution to the Value Inquiry Book Series. I am indebted to Edinboro University for the technical assistance which permitted the final preparation of this manuscript.

One

REQUIEM FOR PROTAGORAS?

Protagoras was an ancient Greek thinker who argued that "Man is the measure of all things." Given the patriarchal nature of his society, this dictum may reflect a sexist point of view, or he may have meant simply that human beings are the measure of all truth.

The air was stale, full of cigarette smoke and clichés. Bonnie Mason's parties were always like this. Everyone who was anyone (or who cared to be anyone) at the university attended her gettogethers.

I loved these occasions. True, the atmosphere was plastic. I was reminded of Mort Sahl's definition of a celebrity: someone who is famous for being well-known. True, every party was no more than an instant replay of the last party. Even the novelties at each gathering wore thin and, after a while, seemed a scheduled part of the routine. Still, I did not attend in order to learn anything profound, meet anyone special, or impress others with my presence. I did love to imagine myself to be the center of this universe, to imagine that all eyes were secretly on me. I attended for the spectacle and the illusion of being above it all. I was not really a part of the spectacle. I was an interested but uninvolved third party. To me, Bonnie Mason's parties were a door to eternity. Several times a semester the door would open, and I was permitted entrance. It was (as Camus might have said) consciousness that made all the difference. Most who came had no idea they were part of this timeless spectacle. How could they? They were oblivious; they lacked lucidity.

Seated directly in front of me were two women. One was a professor of chemistry, and the other was a professor of English. They were arguing about whether it was just to deny federal funds for abortions. The chemistry professor urged that the effect of this denial was to discriminate, as usual, against the poor woman–since the woman of means would find a way to have her abortion. The English professor argued that the argument of the other woman (whom she called "the tube head") was beside the point. She argued that the basic issue concerned the murder of babies and that just because *some* murderers get away with their crime is no reason to subsidize murder in general. Their voices became louder as each retrenched. Yet their heated dispute was barely noticed above the general din caused by scores of intoxicated guests and the steady beat of garbled music in the background.

A fellow who had been sitting next to me and who had also apparently eavesdropped on the abortion debate, nudged my arm and said, “Jesus, you wouldn’t believe the nonsense you hear at such gatherings! Imagine, ‘Is abortion just or unjust?’. People still talk about such subjects as if there were anything to talk about. ‘Justice’ indeed! What crap! Man has finally learned that he is not the center of the universe, yet he still flirts with his absolutes.”

He cut short his speech long enough to verify that he had my attention. Satisfied that he did, he finished his commentary, laughing sarcastically as he concluded, “Imagine how many human beings have died in the name of that hollow word–‘justice.’ In other words, died in the name of a name.”

His dark eyes stared straight into mine as if he was awaiting my response, then shifted back toward the two women as he heaved a deep sigh of exasperation. I had followed his every word and was every bit as interested in this subject as he, but I excused myself from his company, saying that I had to refill my glass, for *in vino veritas*. This seemed to humor him and, to my relief, he did not pursue me. It wasn’t that I did not care for his views about justice, though I didn’t care one bit for his views. A conversation with him would have gone nowhere. Either he would have become impatient when he discovered that I would not “chant” with him, or he would have become downright angry when he learned how little I esteemed his opinion. It wasn’t worth it. He just wanted someone to chime in with him, to echo the “good news for modern, enlightened man” that all morality was relative or subjective. Anyhow, he was disturbing my observations and dragging me back into time. No, I would rather be alone.

I pushed my way to the kitchen, uttering an “excuse me” as I occasionally bumped into someone or stepped on a foot. I had just poured myself a glass of wine when I felt someone tap me on the shoulder. It was the speechmaker.

“Pardon me,” he said, “but don’t you teach at the university? In the Philosophy Department, aren’t you?”

“Yes,” I said, putting a cordial smile on my face while I thought, “Jesus, trapped!”

"That's what I thought," he continued as he stepped by me to pour himself a glass of beer. "You must be quite interested in the subject of justice, or are you one of those 'analytic types'?"

He paused to take a gulp of his beer.

"You know," he continued, "one of those language philosophers, I believe they call them."

I was doubly irritated now. He was bound and determined to consider me a kindred spirit, or at least to show me that he was familiar with modern trends in philosophy. "Why me?" I thought to myself. All I wanted was eternity and the anonymity to enjoy it. Oh well, paradise was lost. I would have to pass time with this fellow.

"I'm not sure how I would classify myself as a philosopher, but yes, I am quite interested in ethics and justice."

"Then," he said, "you overheard those women arguing about abortion. Oh, pardon me," he interrupted himself. "My name is Rudy Barringer. I'm in the Speech Department."

We shook hands. He went on.

"So, you're interested in ethics? I suppose you were also amused by those ladies' argument about the injustices of abortion."

I looked straight into his eyes, then down into my glass of wine.

"No, not really," I replied. "Actually, I find the issue of abortion quite troubling. The truth is that I take questions of justice and injustice quite seriously."

He appeared startled by my response, and for a moment or two we both stared at each other nervously. But all-too-quickly the uneasy silence was broken.

"Really!" he exclaimed. "My goodness, you mean that you think there is some absolute right and wrong, that it is somewhere written in the heavens that abortion is permitted or forbidden? My dear fellow, you are among the last of a dying breed. You must be religious, for otherwise I can't imagine how you could hold such a view. Surely philosophers no longer speak of absolutes without smiling–not after Nietzsche and not after the work of Einstein and Heisenberg!"

He paused and awaited my response. He continued to act nervously, glancing abruptly about the room, as if he felt he might be in the presence of something contagious, as if he might have to dash off at any moment. I couldn't help but smile at his remarks. "How incredibly naive," I thought to myself. He is incredulous over my naiveté, yet he presumes that the latest is the greatest. What a marvel we moderns are. And what snots!

He was looking at me smugly, as if my momentary silence showed that his logic had overwhelmed me. You almost had to respond quickly to people like this. Slow responses were construed as signs of weakness, meaning that you were dull-witted or just mistaken. Such people viewed arguments and conversations as contests or fights. The object was to win, and to do this, you needed to be fast on your feet. You never really talked *with* such people; you fended them off as best you could.

"I have said nothing about heavenly tablets," I said in an impatient tone of voice, "and I don't see that my remarks have any religious implications. People are prone to think that, without God, right and wrong are meaningless ideas, but I do not agree. Even if God exists, I doubt that anything is right simply *because* God decrees that it is. Justice is as independent of God's will as it is of any of our wills. As for what most philosophers think about this these days, I have little idea. In any case, you are not addressing them, but me, so let us pretend that we have not submitted this issue for a vote."

"You have a knack," he said, "of saying astonishing things, not the least of which is your claim that absolute right and wrong can be divorced from God's will. Nevertheless, I won't push that issue now. Do you claim a standard of justice exists which is separate from the standards of justice employed by different individuals, nations, or cultures? A standard which is uniform and which does not vary?"

"Yes," I replied.

"Well," he said in a flip voice, "we certainly perceive no such standard in the world. Instead, what we discover is great variety among what people call 'just'. For example, the bourgeoisie's tidy conception of justice, and the criminal's code of honor, strength, and fidelity, the capitalist conception of justice, and the Marxist conception. Many examples could be cited, yet the point is that we discover in the world not one unvarying standard of justice, but diverse and changing standards. What is one person's poison is another's medicine. We perceive that what people call 'just' varies greatly from one generation to the next. It used to be wrong for people to live together before marriage, but now it is permitted, even encouraged by many. From what we can tell, justice, like beauty, is in the eyes of the beholder."

Someone bumped into me.

"Excuse me," blurted out the fat man. "I was trying to get a refill of beer, and as I'm sure you know, it's every man for himself."

The chubby stranger poured himself a glass of beer, brushed back against me as he left as quickly as he could, chuckling as he moved away.

"I think we had better move, Rudy. We seem to be in everyone's way here."

Rudy nodded his agreement.

"Let's try to edge our way into that bedroom just down the hall. You know, where people leave their coats. We may find some room there."

Again he nodded. We moved slowly toward the hallway, half-stepping, side-stepping–at a snail's pace to avoid collisions which nonetheless were inevitable. A few minutes later we arrived. Except for the bed stacked with a mountain of coats, the room was virtually empty. In one corner was a young couple, probably students, locked in a romantic embrace. Barringer was embarrassed and wanted to look elsewhere, but I convinced him that we were likely to do no better elsewhere and that the students would probably ignore us if we ignored them. Still, we found ourselves trying to be as inconspicuous as possible, positioning ourselves just inside the room's entrance, halfway in and halfway out of the doorway. In this way we avoided the main surge of humanity in the hallway and were barely noticed by the lovers. I picked up our discussion where we had left off.

"You emphasize the fact that what people call 'just' varies so much. Is it the diversity of those things which we call 'just' that makes you think that justice is hopelessly relative or subjective?"

"Yes," he replied. "This is a major part of my thinking."

"Well then, consider this. Cars differ greatly in terms of their appearances. Cadillacs look quite different from Honda Civics, and Corvettes look different from either of them. Yet, though individual cars vary greatly from one another, we still call them cars. Does this mean that the concept of a car is hopelessly relative or subjective or that the concept of a car is as problematic as the concept of justice?"

He did not respond immediately. To my surprise, a few moments passed as he appeared to reflect on what I had said.

"No, the problem is not the mere fact that so many different things are called 'just'. The problem is that so-called 'just things' differ to such a great degree from one another, and one culture may judge that an act, say, having more than one wife, is unjust, whereas another culture may make the opposite judgment. This indicates not the existence of one standard of justice, but several. After all, people never disagree about cars in this way. You don't find one person arguing that a Corvette is a car while someone else argues that it is not."

"True," I replied, "people almost never have any reason to doubt whether what they see is a car. This fact tells us little about the concept of justice. The concept of a car is, for all practical purposes, much less complicated than the concept of justice. Little is at stake for us in judging that something is a car. For example, the judgment that something is (or is not) a car virtually never involves, nor is motivated by strong emotion. The contrary is often true concerning our judgments of justice or injustice. Such judgments typically involve strong emotions. It is hard for human beings to maintain an impartial attitude about whether taking from the rich in order to give to the poor is just, but we can easily lose interest in deciding whether the vehicle before us should be classified as a car, a van, a bus, or something else. Furthermore, our attitudes about justice play a major role in our total outlook on life, as well as how we perceive ourselves. Thus, for example, our conception of justice provides us a means of making sense out of the reality we encounter. The ideal permits us to understand how the world is supposed to behave, whether it does so or not.

It is a mistake to think that the unattainability of the ideal makes it meaningless for us. On the contrary, this transcendence is part of its appeal. The practical nature of the ideal has almost always been overlooked by no-nonsense realists. Human beings have always been willing to regulate their lives (and often deaths) by some ideal, and when they have risked their lives for an ideal, it has never seriously bothered them that the ideal could not be perfectly realized.

Another factor complicates our ease in making judgments about justice: the less we view our behavior as conforming to the ideal norm of just behavior, the more we tend *either* to think poorly of ourselves or to imagine that justice is merely a subjective or relative concept. Thus, many people prefer to eschew the serious nature of moral judgments rather than judge themselves. Self-judgment may require them to be harsh; it may make it difficult to live with themselves. The moral here is just this: powerful factors regarding self-interest are in competition with our understanding of justice. Look at it in this way. No-nonsense realists about morality may not have overcome their childishness. Instead, they may be conceived as children who have learned how to be patient and to calculate ways to gratify their wants and needs. Thus, the realist in us may easily cloud our judgments concerning what is just and unjust."

Barringer stood with his mouth open for a few seconds, as if he had been struck dumb, then he smiled broadly and slapped his hand smartly against his thigh.

"What a bunch of psycho-babble! I can't believe anyone can still spout this quasi-religious nonsense! So the main reason people have trouble discerning what is just and unjust is that they are too selfish to give decency an even break? Isn't this what you're saying? I mean, basically, doesn't it boil down to this: We deny justice only because we are guilty, because we are sinners who refuse to humble ourselves before Righteousness? You moralists make me want to puke!"

"If I understand your reply," I said with a smirk on my face, "you argue that my view is wrong because it is nonsense, quasi-religious, and makes you ill. Charming! It is difficult to refute the realism of the sophisticated soul. But, if you will be patient enough to recall, you implied that the only plausible explanation why people have trouble discerning the nature of justice is that the concept is wholly subjective or relative. In other words, if the concept of justice were objective and clear like that of a car, little difference would arise between people as to what should be called 'just.' Why you insist on calling my view quasi-religious I don't know."

"Because," he shot back, "you speak as though our corrupt nature prevents us from speaking clearly and honestly about justice! This is like arguing that the sinful nature of he who is haughty with pride prevents him from seeing the error of his ways. Also, the standard of justice, you say, is not of this world. Finally, how can we conceive of such ideal justice unless God has decreed and sustained it, a God whose eternal Being bears witness to such absolute values?"

"I suspected as much," I said. "True, a similarity arises between the religious explanation of why people fail to see the Truth and the account I have just presented. But, it is no more than a similarity. I am not arguing that only self-centered people would disagree with me about justice. I am quite sure that many sensitive, well-intentioned people honestly believe that justice is (unfortunately) a subjective or relative matter. As for the standard of justice not being of this world, this may be true without my presupposing any religious view. You doubt this, I presume, because you imagine that if absolute moral rules or commandments exist someone must have authored them. Since these rules or commandments are supposed absolute, human beings are precluded from being their author. Given the nature of these rules or commandments, it is only fitting that their author be a perfect, eternal Being. Isn't this roughly what you have in mind?"

"Yes," he said, "though you needlessly complicate the view. The simple point is that unless an Author exists of absolute moral values, it is pointless to hypothesize their existence."

"But," I said, "you are wrong to place so much importance on the existence of God. May we not suppose that moral rules are discovered and not created? I don't think this forces us to suppose that they are discovered in exactly the same way as the laws of nature are discovered by the scientist. In any case, it is hardly obvious that absolute moral rules must be the willful creation of a divine being. The venerable question of whether something is right *because* it is willed by God, or willed by God *because* it is right, remains. If we insist on the first alternative, we are confronted with the consequence that if God willed something clearly malicious or sadistic, it would thereby become right. If God were, for example, to will that the first-born baby of all future generations was to be slowly burned to death in front of its mother, such an act would thereby become right."

He interrupted me.

"This is absurd! God, if there were a God, would never will such a thing."

"Naturally," I replied, "God would not, because we suppose that God is a perfectly caring and just Being. That is, we imagine that God's very nature prevents God from evil thoughts and deeds. This only reinforces my point. Why do we assume that God would never will the torture of babies and their mothers? Because we suppose such acts are wrong and that God, being perfectly wise, knows this. Hence, God would never will them. There is no getting around this. Either you suppose God is an arbitrary Dictator who is capable of decreeing the most hideous of acts, or you deny this and accept that the standard of right and wrong is independent of God's will. In my mind it is far more plausible and pious to affirm the second alternative. Thus, I would argue that there need be no God if an absolute standard of justice is discoverable."

Barringer's face grew even more flushed.

"Gad!" he exclaimed, "rules which are not empirical generalizations, but are nonetheless *somehow* discovered by us! Absolute rules which are authored by no one! A standard of justice which is not perceived by us, which is not of this world. We are supposed to accept all this. Can you really expect people to countenance such a mysterious and unlikely account of moral concepts? Do you yourself believe it?"

"Well," I replied, "it makes more sense than. . ."

He interrupted.

"Consider this. Suppose we ignore, for the sake of argument, whether justice can be absolute when rational people have such varying ideas of what justice is. How, in your view, do we come by this absolute idea of justice? At least we can *experience* justice if it is relative as I have argued. But justice conceived as absolute and unchanging is something we never perceive. The origin of this high and mighty concept you propose remains suspect. So far as we know, such a concept–if indeed we are familiar with such a concept–may well be the product of our human imagination. We can imagine unreal things which never change and are dependent upon no one's perspective. No one doubts the richness of human fantasy, especially for good fairies and for evil goblins. However, if this concept of justice you have been trying to peddle originates in our imagination, it will again turn out to be a subjective or relative concept–relative to the power of our individual imagination or the collective fancy of our culture."

"Far too much," I said, "is made of where we gain our ideas of right and wrong. You argue, for example, that if justice is as I claim, it certainly is nothing we perceive or experience in the world. You say that unless we can trace our concept back to our experience of the world, the concept's objectivity is doubtful. Such a view is ancient in its influence on human thought. It is a hardheaded realism according to which the perceivable world is the Standard of objectivity. Thus, you may reason: Imaginary stars are seen only by some; such stars are subjective. Real stars, on the other hand, are seeable by all and are, therefore, objective. This realistic view is as naive as it is misguided. It is paraded under the persuasive banner of common sense, but it is–if followed consistently–inimical to common sense.

Suppose we were to say that all concepts must be derived from what we perceive (if they are to be considered dependable). What, then, should we say of our concept of time? Time is not something we perceive. We can perceive clocks, calendars, motion, change, and we can pay attention to our experience of change–but we never perceive time. As Augustine long ago pointed out, it is a mistake to identify time with change or motion, since any change and any motion occur in time and are measurable within time. Let us carefully ponder the consequences of maintaining that all reliable concepts must be derived from some perceivable phenomenon.

Either our concept of time is reliable, or it is not. Suppose it is not. If not, common sense and hardheaded realism are in a quandary. If our concept of time is not reliable, then our very idea of the sequence past-present-future is jeopardized. Our belief in past events, in our own past, and in history may be nothing more than a fiction produced by our imagination. Our judgments that some people are older than others, that events endure for a period of time, that light travels at a certain speed would hinge upon an undependable concept. Neither common sense nor science is coherent without our presupposing that time is objective and dependable. If our concept of time is not dependable, then neither is common sense or science.

On the other hand, suppose that our concept of time is reliable. If so, then given our previous working assumptions, it must be derived from something we perceive. Yet our concept of time is not derived in this way. This would imply that our concept of time is not reliable. Consequently, we are confronted with the following dilemma. Either common sense and science rest on nonsense, or not all of our reliable concepts need be derived from what we perceive. I shall not attempt to speak for you, but for my part, I am far more certain of the first alternative's falsehood than I am of the falsehood of the second alternative. I would argue that we have good reason not only for supposing that objective concepts need not be derived from our perceptual experience, and that the viability of common sense and science depends upon this being a fact."

Rudy had been glaring at me for some time. Now his countenance softened into a perplexed look.

"Yes, I think I see your point," he said. "Maybe you are right about time. Perhaps we don't get this idea from anything we perceive. I say 'perhaps' because I am not altogether certain that time isn't subjective and relative. Think of the different time zones in this world; what time it is depends upon which zone you happen to be in, and the method for keeping the world's time is largely an arbitrary human convention that could be done otherwise. Think, for example, of daylight savings versus standard time. And I also think. . ."

I interrupted.

"Nevertheless, the different time zones belie a more fundamental idea of time, and this basic idea is not affected by your remarks. Without our conception of the sequence past-present-future, and without our conception of time as the 'master index' (the fourth-dimensional container) of all worldly things, the convention of the time zones would be quite meaningless. Our absolute idea of time looms in the background of our relative ideas of time."

"Well, perhaps you are right about this," Barringer replied. "I'm not saying you are right, but let's suppose you are. What good is an absolute standard of time if that standard always becomes relativized when it is applied. I mean, who cares if there is–in some sense–an absolute standard of time? The truth is that, in human experience, Rocky Mountain Standard Time is not Eastern Standard Time. In human terms, what time it is and whether it is day or night depend upon where you happen to be. If absolute justice is like absolute time, as is plausible in this respect, then its ethereal existence is of little value to human beings. As with time, what is just and unjust in human terms will depend upon who you are and where you happen to be. Thus, we will have the master's justice and the slave's justice, the rich person's justice and the poor person's justice, and so on. Absolute justice, like absolute time, will remain buried in the shadows of abstraction, a nebulous and hollow specter!"

In an odd way, I had made some progress with Mr. Barringer. Now, at least, he was not questioning the existence of a non-subjective standard of justice, but was merely arguing that something was inevitably lost in translation when we applied this standard of justice to human affairs.

"You remind me," I said with a smile, "of that ancient sophist who argued that either there is no Truth, or if there is, we cannot know it. Both of you are too quick to be skeptical. Room exists for some relativity in judgments about justice without there being both a slave's and a master's justice. Consider the relationship between justice and equality. As I see it, justice does not amount to treating everyone equally–not if we interpret 'equality' in a strict sense. It would be an awful blunder to treat a premeditated mass murderer in the same way we would treat a girl who had accidentally shot her father while on a hunting trip.

Of course, someone will say that justice amounts to treating 'like cases alike.' It is notoriously difficult to pin down the exact and general flavor of this recipe, but I suppose that it does capture the mood of an important part of justice. "Treating like cases alike" can serve as our unswerving standard of justice even though what we judge to be just in particular circumstances varies greatly. It may be just for people who are quite poor and unable to get work to steal in order to support their family, but it may also be very unjust for people who are quite rich to shoplift a candy bar from a grocery store. There is, and should be, a different justice for the rich and for the poor. Not only are there "different justices," but there must be if we are to be moral. This fact in no way demeans the concept of justice, but illustrates the immense flexibility of a concept which people–including yourself–often speak of as if it were unyieldingly rigid.

On this score, as on many others, I argue that justice has gotten bad press–not from the ignorant masses, but from the educated elite. In order to be accepted in some intellectual circles, you have to take for granted the relativity of values. Thus, the foundations of value have been assaulted by the very foe who could do the most damage. Formerly, we could combat the rabble's egocentricity: against their eyes and ears, we could oppose arguments. Alas, now it is almost too late for this. Now some of the educated preach that the arguments are also on the rabble's side. Some say it is no longer reasonable to believe in the objectivity of value. This, they say, is the good news for modern folks. Ironically, the rabble's own convictions, as well as their innate distrust of intellectuals, have so far prevented them from accepting this good news. Whether these ethical nihilists are actually reporting the modern news or just passing along ancient gossip is an open question."

We stared at one another. He seemed nervous, or perhaps annoyed. The hand in which he held his glass of beer shook steadily, and his voice wavered slightly as he spoke.

"This is absolutely incredible! Not only do you defend absolute values, but you act as if those who differ with you are undermining civilization! But you are thereby opposing the spirit of calm, no-nonsense, scientific thinking, and such thinking is responsible for the very maintenance and advancement of civilization. Such a hubbub over the alleged existence of an absolute standard of justice–a concept whose origin is extremely mysterious! You admit you cannot account for how we derive it. All this does not suit philosophy but smacks of mysticism."

"It is clear," I said, "you still find my view unbelievable, but accusing me of being unscientific and mystical is to no avail. If my view is mistaken, surely there must be better ways of revealing its flaws than such name-calling and innuendo. Scientific thinking is not the only kind of thinking, and scientific values are not the only values to be considered. In any event, to criticize moral concepts for being unscientific is (to steal a phrase from Wittgenstein) like criticizing a work bench because it cannot fly. Such criticism is inappropriate here. After all, we may boil down most of the usual criticisms of moral concepts into the following: they are not empirical but metaphysical. But, as I have argued about time, science itself rests upon a metaphysics. Science relies upon concepts whose origins are as difficult to pin down in our experience as they are essential to science. I have concentrated on the concept of time, but many others could be mentioned.

Consider, for example, the concept of value itself. We could easily get carried away in our critique of moral values and claim that the concept of value is, in itself, a subjective and relative concept. But as soon as we take this further step (and why shouldn't we condemn other concepts of value if we are willing to condemn the concept of moral value?), what are we to say of the value of science or of scientific values? We must conclude that either science rests upon no values (which is ridiculous), or the value of science is entirely a subjective or relative matter, which again threatens the claim of science to be objective. There is no getting around it; science needs unscientific concepts just as much as we moralists. Thus, any rejection of the concept of justice on the grounds that it is unscientific, unobservable, or intangible is bound also to imply a rejection of common sense and science."

"Hogwash!" he burst out. "Philosophy has not changed much since the days when old Socrates was given poison for being such a damned nuisance! You begin by affirming the absurd, then take refuge in abstract arguments and gobbledegook in order to defend yourself. Science and common sense hardly stand or fall with the notion of some other-worldly justice or philosopher's heaven. Common sense deals with facts, with concrete realities, things a person can see and grasp. As for science, its accomplishments are legion and apparent to all. By comparison, what may we say of morality conceived as a set of absolute values? What are its accomplishments? Virtually zero, my friend! To accept such absolutes, we must close our eyes and ears, take refuge in shadowy abstractions, and ignore common sense. Furthermore, people are just as self-centered and savage as they have always been. Fathers and mothers may go to church and preach decency to their children, but they make sure that their children realize you've got to look out for number one if you're to fit into this world. . .if you're to be *sensible*. We have invented marvelous new weapons for maiming and destroying our enemies, and we can even destroy the whole world if we choose. No, science and common sense will long outlive your ghostly Justice. People have never taken such notions seriously–not adults–and they never shall."

"My dear fellow," I said as I gritted my teeth, "you remain excellent as a speech giver. I fear you pay no attention to my arguments. You affirm that the fate of science and common sense is not linked to that of Justice, but this was never an issue between us. I full-well realize that people can continue to scoff at absolute values while taking science and common sense seriously. This is no surprise. It is no more surprising that many Christians scoff at magic and superstition, yet firmly believe that Jesus and Moses performed many miracles. I wouldn't say they are hypocrites, just that they haven't thought things through. What I was arguing, if you recall, is that people don't realize what they imply by attacking the objectivity of moral values. They don't realize that..."

He interrupted.

"Frankly, my good man, I don't much care what your point was. I am sorry to appear rude, but the truth is that nothing you have said has changed my mind in the slightest. Some of your arguments I followed, although they did not persuade me. Some of your arguments I could not follow–largely because they were unnecessarily abstruse. Really, you should wise-up and confront your fellow human being honestly rather than playing hide and seek in these effeminate arguments. If you want to prove something to me, *show* me your evidence; show me the facts. You prove nothing about the objectivity of justice by falling back on these theoretical arguments about the nature of time and so on. Anyone can prove anything if they stick to theorizing and speculation. What we need here is not theory, but facts. Unhappily, facts are the one thing you refuse to use in making your case–

which I suppose is usual for philosophers. In any case, I don't begrudge you keeping your head in the clouds, but forgive me if I cut short our discussion. I see a woman friend of mine who has been trying to get my attention for some time now. I think you and I have reached a stalemate. Nice talking with you."

He moved quickly away toward the kitchen, turning once briefly to smile at me. Before he disappeared from my sight, I saw him stop by a tall woman with blonde hair. She smiled broadly, and the two of them quickly vanished into the crowd. I was both relieved and exasperated. It was a relief to be rid of my interrogator, but having been drawn into this unwanted conversation, my adrenalin was flowing and I wanted to continue the argument. I loathed Barringer's pigheadedness and shallow nature! A cocktail party priest! I sank into depression as I continued the argument in my imagination.

The modern attitude did not seem much different from the ancient one, save, that we were scientific. At bottom, the conviction remained the same: what is real must be what is obvious to most people, and this amounted to what most could see and touch. How remarkable that reality "happened" to favor the common person and democracy. . .! This intoxication with and worship of the visible had deeply concerned Plato. He blamed the nihilism of his culture on such sentiments. Perhaps he had gone too far in opposing the obvious and the common, but surely he was right to have opposed them. The nihilistic progression runs as follows. In numbers there is Truth, hence the public's perspective defines Reality. The public knows that the paradigm of reality is what we can see and touch. If we look to the visible and tangible as our guide to value, we perceive variation and difference, not uniformity. Thus, the overall conclusion can be drawn (using our safety-in-numbers indicator of truth): what we can agree on is that *no one is right*. The seed of profound nihilism lies here.

To combat such nihilism, Plato stood the obvious on its head. "No," he insisted, "the most real and the most valuable is not what we see and touch. Indeed, what we see and touch is the least real, the least valuable. Truth is not given to us; we must seek it out. And the truth is, it is not easy to find." The public was not only wrong, but they had managed to reverse the true order of things. Outrageous? Naturally. But how else can you deal with a collective will which demands that reality be democratic and not too difficult? At bottom, the sentiment is egocentric and childish. We must not cater to such sentiment, especially when it is so powerful and self-assured, and when it survives in adult form. We must be firm, and sometimes we have to confront one extreme with another in order to achieve moderation.

I still couldn't believe it. Somehow, it had been "discovered" that moral values were hopelessly relative, and also that the only real things were what we could see and touch. How had we "discovered" this? This is an immense–perhaps infinite–universe into which we are thrown. Wouldn't it be surprising if it turned out that reality had only enough room for what we could see and touch? Granted that many do not find this surprising, but how did we discover this? By looking and touching the visible and the tangible, you say? Noble "discovery!" And what of the imaginable and the thinkable? How had we discovered that they were unreal, or not as real as
the tangible? Why, because they could not be seen and touched! The virtue of such merry-go-round logic must be its simplicity. I was reminded of the vain king who believed that he was the fairest king of all. In order to prove this to himself, he had his bedroom lined wall-to-wall with mirrors so that he might be able to watch himself as often as possible.

I was jolted out of my reverie when someone abruptly brushed my arm, spilling my wine all over my pants.

"Damn it!" I shouted. "Why don't you watch. . ."

I stopped my tirade as quickly as I had launched it. Standing in front of me was a short woman, whose long brown hair fell nearly to the small of her back.

"I'm terribly sorry," she said in a soft, faltering voice. "Please excuse me. I'm very sorry; really I am. It's just that the man behind me lost his balance, shoving me into you. Really, forgive me."

No rage was left in me. I saw only the large, oval green eyes and the soft, polite smile. Suddenly, I was aware not only of her sweet perfume, but also of the fog of cigarette smoke, the steady drone of the crowd, and a potpourri of other snaps and crackles. Once again I was relaxed. I was removed. . .and lost to time.

Two

SOME MISCONCEPTIONS ABOUT MORALITY

1. Is Morality a Religious Affair?

People commonly associate morality with religion. This is not surprising, since all religions preach adherence to a moral code. We hear "thou shall do this" and "thou shall not do that." We learn that joyous rewards and hellish penalties are at stake according to the will of God, and we see to it that our children hear the same story. Since many religious teachings are unnatural in what they require of us, such as loving our enemies and blessing those that curse us, moral commitment seems to involve a belief in the supernatural. Thus, many people think that we cannot be moral, or not very deeply moral, unless we have religious faith (to provide guidelines for living our life). Typically, people believe that God is the cornerstone of all moral value, and objective morality could not exist if God did not exist. Consequently, atheistic existentialists like Sartre have argued that moral values are created rather than discovered by us. On the other hand, Christian thinkers argue that since God is not dead, we should turn to God as the foundation of moral value.

The view that moral value is determined by the divine will is ancient. In his dialogue, the *Euthyphro*, Plato examines and rejects a similar view: that piety is determined by what the gods love. Although he does not specifically consider whether moral right is determined by the gods' will, Plato probably would have rejected such a view. His argument against defining piety in terms of the gods' will applies equally well against defining morality in such terms. Furthermore, if Plato rejects the notion that piety–a religious concept–is dependent upon the divine will, it is unlikely that he would make morality depend upon the divine attitude. We have little reason to think that religion is essential to morality, and there are dangers in thinking that the two are inseparable.

Let us avoid a misunderstanding. I am not going to argue for or against the existence of God. I am not denying that God, if God exists, would be supremely relevant as a guide to right action. As God is normally conceived, God is infinitely loving and wise. Consequently, God would inevitably want us to do what is right, and God would inevitably know what is right for us. God would know the best way to communicate moral knowledge to us and, being all-powerful, would succeed. On these grounds alone, we would be warranted in heeding God's will in matters of right and wrong. Since God is perfect (in contrast with our many limitations), we would be foolish to ignore God's will.

Is something right because God wills it so? Consider the consequences. If something is right solely due to God's willing it so, then what if God willed that lying and cheating were right? Suppose God willed that normally it was right for us to deceive and cheat our neighbors. Then it would be right to lie to and cheat our neighbors. What if God willed that we torture infants with red hair? Would it, then, be right to torture such infants? Apparently so, if God's will determines the rightness of things.

But, you may say to yourself, such hypothetical circumstances are absurd. God would never will that we lie and cheat, much less that we torture little children. Quite so, but why would God not will such things? Surely the answer is: because God is a perfectly good and perfectly wise Being. In other words, God's own character would prevent God from behaving in evil or foolish ways. The interesting point is that God's character is such that God–being perfectly wise–never wills what is wrong (but always what is right). Let us express this relation clearly: something is not right because God wills it; the reverse is true. God wills something because that thing is right. If people say it is because God wills us to love our neighbors that loving our neighbors is right, what they say (if anything true) may be paraphrased as follows: Because a Being who has perfect moral intentions and who knows perfectly what is right wills this–loving our neighbors is right.

It is presumptuous for the faithful to pass judgment upon what God would or would not will for us to do! If God has so far willed that we not commit adultery, does this mean that God will not or cannot have a change of mind about this? Who among the faithful is fearlessly prepared to say that God cannot or will not alter God's commandments? Surely, it is a great sin of pride to pronounce limitations on God's will. Neither can the faithful argue that God would never will anything awful, much less what appears awful to us. The Bible informs us of God's condemning, assisting, and directly carrying out awful acts (for example, mass slaughters of the enemy) against human beings. Consider how God allowed Job to be tested by immense suffering, or consider God's command to Abraham that he kill his only son Isaac. Such a judgment about God's limitations is no pious venture for the faithful. There is no reason for us to be certain that God would not decree hideous evils (at least, as far as we mortals can tell) *if* one makes God's will the sole standard of right and wrong.

The issue here is not purely academic. Dangers exist in supposing that religion is essential to morality. We are not splitting hairs in insisting that something would not be right because God wills it, but willed by God because it is right. Intelligent and sensitive people too often shy away from ethics due to a narrow-mindedness and intolerance which they associate with making moral judgments. They loathe "morally" judging people where this involves a self-righteous meddling in others' private affairs. They view such moralizing as unwarranted and often hypocritical. As it happens, organized religion has encouraged this kind of zealous and harsh judging of others. Recall the biblical story of the woman who was being stoned by indignant citizens and Jesus' admonition to the zealots that only the non-sinners among them should cast a stone.

This story illustrates another reason why sensitive people have been put off by moralizing. The woman's transgression in the story was sexual in nature. In the Western world, religious moral codes have been preoccupied with sexual mores. To the extent that our Western culture is a Judeo-Christian culture, this has meant that common "morality" has also been obsessed with sexual mores. This obsession has been so intense that, other than obeying the law and being generally honest, morality has been almost exclusively identified with observing sexual taboos. Any mention of morality and immorality is almost certain to make us think first of adultery, promiscuity, pre-marital sex, virginity, marriage, or the family. It is this kind of moral obsessiveness and narrow-mindedness which offends the sensibilities of many.

Religion need not involve a narrow-minded approach to morality. Nor need it involve self-righteous meddling in others' private affairs. But religion has a marked tendency to manifest its moral commitments in precisely these directions. Therefore, to the extent that religion is associated with morality, to that extent morality is likely to get a bad name among many people who ought to be most drawn to it. The last people we should risk turning away from morality are those who are intelligent and sensitive. Yet, a real danger of wedding religion to morality is that we thereby run the risk of alienating such people.

Another danger lurks in holding that God's will makes things right or wrong. Such a view reinforces authoritarianism and anti-rationalism. If the foundation of moral value is God's willfulness, then we should act morally for basically the same reason that a dictator's subjects should obey the dictator–for fear of angering the dictator. Under the authoritarian conception of God and morality–God has the power, God made the rules, and God made the ballpark in which we must play. We are in no position to question God. This view is anti-rational because it winds up basing morality on power. Right and wrong are born of an act of Will, and they are legitimized and sustained by the infinite power of that Will. Right and wrong are not discovered, but created. Thus, ultimately morality is an invention. This invention, contrary to human inventions, deserves to be taken seriously due to the awesome consequences of disobeying God. Authoritarianism is based on the reverence and fear of power.

2. Intolerance and the Reverence of Authority

Acceptance of the religious authoritarian's model of morality naturally reinforces its application in other areas as well. Thus, parents may believe that the reason their children should do as they say is because they have said so. A teacher may use the same authoritarian model in the classroom, the employer with employees, the football coach with the team, and so on. The authoritarian outlook on life and values has a double edge. Authoritarians are just as prone to blind obedience as they are to absolute command. There are far more sheep than wolves among the authoritarians. "The authorities know best" used to be the predominant attitude among college students, and it still enjoys wide acceptance. Students believed that administrators and teachers were surrogate parents and that to question their authority was bad manners. In the realm of politics, many citizens–and even in the United States–still hold an excessively deferential attitude toward government leaders. Many citizens still believe that our leaders know best, even when the outward evidence continually points to the opposite conclusion. The outward disparity is handled by assuming that our leaders are in possession of relevant information which we lack. The tremendous faith that such a stand requires borders on a religious conviction and is illustrative of the authoritarian temperament.

In the area of employee-employer relations, we can also find examples of the submissive authoritarian attitude. Some employees believe that their employer knows best to such an extent that they identify more with the employer's fate than with that of fellow employees–even more than with their own fate. Consider the following case. At a midwestern university, the Philosophy Department faculty were trying to decide whether to use graduate assistant funds to help create a new faculty position or to keep the graduate assistant positions at their current number. The philosophy graduate students met to discuss strategy. Some argued that the teaching assistants should strike in the fall if the faculty reduced the current number of assistantships. One senior graduate assistant spoke firmly against a strike, arguing that the faculty knew best and should have the right to make such decisions. Another suggestion was that all assistants should commit a small percentage of each of their next year's monthly checks to help subsidize the student who might be laid-off (not knowing which of them might be the one). It was also agreed that this plan would be passed only if the vote in favor was unanimous. The plan was defeated. The same graduate assistant who had argued that "faculty knew best" voted against it. Ironically, it was that same dissenting person whose assistantship was canceled by the faculty.

At bottom, authoritarianism reveres and promotes power, not morality. Identifying religion with morality, and God's will with righteousness, reinforces the authoritarian spirit, and such a mistaken identification is at odds with the ends of justice. Just as there is great wisdom in separating church and state, so too there is wisdom in separating the moral from the holy.

Another misconception about morality lies in thinking that the moral attitude is the same as what I call "moral imperialism." This mistaken identification sours many sensitive souls on the need for being "moral." By "moral imperialism," I mean the attitude that your cultural values *or* your purely personal values must be everyone's values. Moral imperialists will not rest until they have brought to submission all "barbaric" customs and values–those which differ enough from theirs to offend them. In this way they are no different than the ugly American, the ugly Greek, the ugly Roman, the ugly Japanese, or any other representative of imperialistic chauvinism. The moral imperialist is a zealous missionary who will not stop short of converting the heathen, or of letting them know how disgusting their heathen ways are. Thus, the ugly American may make clear when travelling abroad that basic decency and superior values are on the side of fast food and fluency in English. In any case, if another's games, eating habits, sexual mores, or political institutions contradict the moral imperialist's cultural or personal values, this will be construed as proof of the other's uncivilized nature.

Although moral imperialism may involve clashes of cultural values, it can also involve value clashes within the same general culture. In American culture, such conflicts have often occurred concerning sexual values. Moral imperialism has been common in mainstream, puritanical, Christian culture. Attempts, especially among young people, to broaden the areas of permissible sex have been firmly condemned as symptoms of moral decadence. The slogan of many young people in the late 1960s, "Make Love, Not War," was viewed by many Americans as almost satanic advice. Moral imperialism may manifest itself in more individualistic ways; it need not involve a clear-cut clash of cultures or subcultures. Many of us, I suspect, have known people who have the domineering attitude that their way of doing things is always the right way. If they dislike foreign films, then it is stupid to go to foreign films. If they prefer some types of cars, foods, wines, or homes, then any other sort of preference is simply stupid or uncouth. As with other forms of moral imperialism, the imperialist at this level exhibits self-righteousness, inflexibility, fervor, zealousness, and intolerance.

Moral imperialism is far from being the moral point of view, and it is a shame that the two attitudes have often been identified with one another. Perhaps the two become linked as a result of the vocal nature of moral imperialists, for they normally carry around their own soap box and pedestal, and perhaps because the authority of religious institutions has often been a haven for moral imperialism. Whatever the reason, moral imperialism is a harsh and unwarranted intolerance, and as such, it is an immoral attitude.

Moral imperialism is flawed in three basic ways. (1) It conflates strength of conviction with moral genuineness. Feeling strong revulsion at the very thought of some practices (perhaps sexual acts), is taken as proof that their commitment is not only sincere, but moral. (2) It often involves the assumption that their cultural values, institutions, and practices are *the* values of morality. Here a mistake is made, for cultural values are not the same thing as moral values.

(3) Moral imperialism errs in accepting the principle that the end justifies the means. It is not always right (even if you are right) to insist that you are right. Sometimes when you are right and the other person is wrong, it is kinder and more just to allow the other person to be wrong. Suppose, for example, you have a friend who thinks the world of someone. Your friend is wholly convinced the person is kind and unselfish, but you know the other one is notorious for giving this surface impression in order to use people for selfish ends. Suppose you have tried to tell your friend about this misjudgment, but your friend goes so far as to suggest that your real motive for criticism is envy. To press your case here might only hurt your friend's feelings and damage your friendship. It might be best to shut up. Suppose, to take another example, you have a friend who is damaging his or her health by smoking cigarettes. Even if it would be better for your friend to kick this habit, it does not follow that you should badger him or her to do so. For one matter, you might have some personal bad habits that you would rightfully resent being lectured about by others. Hypocrisy is a constant danger, especially for a "moral" zealot. An initial or occasional expression of concern, especially if done politely and non-abrasively, is a different matter altogether. However difficult it may be to define precisely the border-line between badgering and legitimate expressions of concern, a difference does exist between the two.

Two wrongs never make a right, and the danger is that your effort to correct a wrong may itself be wrong. Even if it is unwise and immoral for people to voluntarily harm themselves, it might be equally wrong in some cases for others to intrude. Since none of us is infallible, and since so little in life is in our control–it is only fair that we be allowed peace of mind in conducting our personal affairs. Having such peace of mind involves being allowed to make foolish choices where our choices affect only (or mainly) ourselves. This involves being allowed to deceive ourselves a bit about the wisdom of our choices. Being admonished by others for our (allegedly) foolish behavior constitutes an attack on our character, and such attacks are bound to do violence to our sense of dignity. Doing violence to anything requires justification, and in cases where the person's only (supposed) folly is self-harm, many cases may arise where the attack on the person's dignity is not justified.

3. Moral "Fact": How Can We Decide?

Another misconception about ethical issues is that, contrary to factual issues, something is particularly hard or peculiar about knowing what is right and what is wrong. This conviction takes two basic forms.

First, people imagine that a serious study of ethics is useful only if it will allow definite yes or no answers to all questions of moral right and wrong. They likewise imagine that a subject matter is objective only if it allows a yes or no answer to questions about reality. But, as they will argue, ethical issues are notoriously vague or ambiguous. Take, for example, the prohibition against killing. It is fine to pronounce killing immoral, but does this mean that all killing is murder? Must we not allow for self-defense? What about killing other animals and plants for our survival, or to enhance our standard of living? If our side is the loser in a war, our killing will be called unprovoked, savage, or worse. But if our side is victorious, our killing will be called honorable, self-defense, and heroic. Gang fights are unnecessary and barbaric; gang killings are murder. Nation fights are inevitable and necessary to defend civilization. The mass slaughter of war is. . .well, war is hell. What about abortion? Some look at the facts and argue that the fertilized egg is a human being with the same right to life as you or me. Therefore, they conclude that abortion is murder. Others look at the same facts and argue that the fertilized egg is more fish than human and has no human rights. They conclude that abortion is hardly murder. Since reality is not itself contradictory, vague or ambiguous, the fuzziness and contradictory nature of moral "reality" must be due to its subjective origin–the fluctuating horizons of human perception and subjective preference. If right and wrong are not matters of black and white, but shades of gray–this is because moral "reality" is merely subjective reality.

But this way of thinking exaggerates the fuzzy and indefinite nature of moral questions. While some moral issues are hard to decide, many moral issues are clear-cut. Stealing is normally wrong, and that's it. Only extreme circumstances–stealing to keep one's family from starving–can morally excuse stealing. Lying is normally wrong, and that's the end of the matter. If I tell you a lie simply to take revenge on a mutual acquaintance, my lie is wrong–period. Killing people is normally wrong, and that's that. If I want your wife and kill you in order to have her for my lover, my act is wrong–period. Determining right and wrong can be as clear as a mountain morning.

Genuinely perplexing moral questions exist. Abortion is a case in point. A sensitive soul can struggle mightily with this issue, yet remain unsure whether (and under what circumstances) having an abortion is right. The theology of some people tells them that abortion is unequivocally and categorically wrong because it is murder. Similarly, some people claim that abortion is unequivocally and categorically permissible from a moral point of view. This group may argue that having an abortion is basically no different than having an ingrown toenail removed. As I see it, the ability to pronounce such definitive answers on this issue indicates a lack of thought or sensitivity. A person should have–if not an absolute right–great latitude in deciding what to do with his or her body. The decision regarding the legitimacy of abortion should not be left mainly or exclusively in the hands of men. It is not right to have laws and customs concerning abortion which, in effect, preclude only poor women from having abortions. Yet, the ominous possibility lingers that abortion may be homicide or murder. Is the fetus (fertilized egg or zygote) a human being, or is it something non-human or pre-human? Perhaps the fetus is a potential human being, and we may be wrong to kill what is potentially human. Perhaps the fetus is human, and the real issue is whether the mother's killing the fetus is ever justifiable as self-defense.

The sensitive, moral person wants to be fair to women, and does not want to base judgments solely on gut feelings, religious fanaticism, or ignorance of the facts. But neither does the sensitive moral person want to condone murder or unnecessary killing. The abortion issue invites us to fathom the concept of a person or a human being. What is a person? What is a human being? We would like science to help us decide, but science is not able to help much. Science can give us precise descriptions of the stages of fetal development, but unless we already know what a person is, we won't know whether any given stage qualifies as a person. We count the newly born baby as a person with the same right to life that we enjoy. Yet how different is the newly born baby from the creature which had just a few moments ago inhabited the mother's womb? We are tempted to say the difference is that the newly born baby exists independently of the mother–yet this raises new questions. First, though the baby exists outside the mother, does the baby have an "independent" existence? The baby will quickly die if not cared for by others. Second, if this is an essential criterion of being a person with the right to life, what about severely ill or handicapped people? What about the many elderly who are highly dependent on others for their very existence? Surely, in these latter cases we are dealing with persons, not non-human or sub-human entities as the logic about fetuses would indicate.

What exactly is involved in the concept of a human being? Can we describe this adequately in purely physical terms, or do mental features also need to be included? Is it any more plausible to claim that a human being is a body infused (at fertilization by God) with a soul than to say a human being is anything with a certain genetic structure? When you think of concrete people you know, when you focus on your friends or family–aren't both of these definitions quite lifeless and hollow? Even if human beings always possess a definite genetic structure, surely there is more to being human than that. This is like defining a star in terms of its heat. The difficulties of mapping our concept of a human being, as well as other obstacles to our settling the abortion issue, could be drawn out in greater length. The point here is to acknowledge a case where deciding a moral issue is quite difficult.

Finally, we face the issue of male hypocrisy. Suppose a male really is unclear whether to judge that the developing fetus is a human being with the same right to life we associate with innocent human beings. Can he then judge the mother morally wrong for having an abortion when he might make the same choice if he were a woman with an unwanted pregnancy? It is far easier for the male to adopt a firm stand against abortion–knowing that he will not have to endure the same hardship as a woman whose pregnancy is unwanted. But this is to run the real risk of moral hypocrisy. The point is that even *if* abortion is always wrong, many (if not all) males may not be in a position personally to morally condemn such action. This is the position I find myself in, and this is why I cannot bring myself to declare abortion morally wrong for women.

A careful examination of the abortion issue reveals that it may be out of the question to say whether abortion is definitely right or definitely wrong. The complexities surrounding this issue are immense. This does not mean that we cannot arrive at a reasonable decision about the morality or immorality of abortion, but it does indicate that the solution will not be simple or clear-cut.

Not only are great social issues like abortion or mercy-killing exceedingly hard to resolve. Specific moral decisions made by individuals in the solitariness of their life may also involve great ambiguity and prove maddening to resolve. This is likely to happen whenever we are confronted with a cluster of moral values we accept, yet which give contradictory advice about what we should do. Abortion is a classic example of this, but many ambiguities are present in the mundane situations of our lives. Lovers know this better than anyone else. In deciding, for example, whether you should stay or leave, it often seems that there is no right way to proceed. You try to sort out and weigh the priorities of your various obligations, and in the end they swim before your eyes. On some such occasions, the best decision you are able to reach is a stalemate–yet you feel you must go beyond this. Such are the frustrations of life and love.

Each of us can think of our own examples of this point, but here are a few more. We give special privileges to physically handicapped persons because, due to their undeserved disabilities and resulting special needs, we believe they deserve special help. Thus, even though it can greatly inconvenience us as we rush to the store only to discover the most convenient parking spots are reserved for the handicapped, we believe that their needs deserve to take precedence over ours. Many of our tax dollars go toward funding special projects for the handicapped even though most of us are in no way to blame for their handicapped condition. Such spending and special treatment create little controversy.

Another area parallels our special treatment of the physically disabled, yet causes great public outcry. I refer to Affirmative Action plans to assist minorities and women (victimized by past and present patterns of discrimination) to compete equally with white males for educational and employment opportunities. Here, we encounter indignant allegations of reverse discrimination. We find impassioned arguments that it is unfair or unreasonable to penalize innocent white folks of the present for the injustices done to women and minorities of the past by sexism and racism. We are reminded that in education and employment only ability should count–not skin color or gender. Affirmative Action, so the argument goes, is a case of trying to rectify injustice by being unjust–a moral no-no.

I will not pretend to resolve this controversy. Indeed, it may be that this issue is not rationally resolvable because of the complexity and ambiguities which swirl around the rationale for Affirmative Action. Nevertheless, I believe Affirmative Action is morally defensible, and this issue invites us to consider how justice relates to individual well-being versus the general good.

No doubt, present and past patterns of sexism and racism have greatly handicapped most women and members of minority groups. Consider the racist effects on black citizens of America. The legacy of slavery and racism against blacks includes "self-degrading" messages such as: it is only the exceptional black that is both hard working and intelligent (which destroys self-confidence). Other effects include destruction of the link of blacks to their cultural past (breaking up slave families and giving them new names) and destruction of their ability to improve their lot through political participation and power (via "legal" and extra-legal impediments). They have been denied access to an equally good education, limiting blacks to hard labor and low-income jobs. This guaranteed that their economic resources would make them second-class competitors for other resources in our society. Racist practices and attitudes have guaranteed that for black citizens it will be the "exceptional exception" who earns a decent living or gets ahead in our white middle-class society. If being black in America hasn't been a severe handicap in all these ways (psychologically, socially, politically, and economically) for the great majority of black Americans, it is hard to imagine any meaning to "having a handicap." Blacks haven't just been riding in the back of the bus; they've been far back down the road running to catch the bus. Since half of the black population has been female, the added blow of sexism has doubly ravaged African-American women.

Ethically speaking, African-Americans did not deserve to be enslaved or discriminated against because of their skin color. There can also be no doubt that blacks do not deserve to start from a disadvantaged position just because of the effects of past or current racism against them. The legacy of racism indicates that blacks have suffered and continue to suffer injustice in our society, due to their conspicuous skin color. Morality requires that injustice should be corrected, so far as is possible. Hence, we encounter the idea of Affirmative Action schemes as a means of compensating for the unfair position–as competitors–which most blacks are placed in our society. The general idea is that since being black is already one strike against them, or automatically puts most blacks "a few" steps back of the starting line, why not use *the very fact which has handicapped them* in our society, namely, their blackness, to give them a leg up? Why not give blacks a positive handicap as a way of ensuring their equal opportunity to compete with white Americans? What could be more relevant or more fair? Even golfers gets a "handicap." The system is designed to help level the competitive playing field, and works as follows. Professional golfers are expected to play the course in par, so only amateurs receive handicaps. Suppose par for a golf course is 72 strokes, and suppose an amateur golfer averages a score of 85 when playing on this course. This amateur will then be assigned a handicap of, say, 10. They are never given the entire difference between par and their average score. If the amateur enters a competitive golf tournament, this means that 10 strokes will be deducted from any score he or she shoots on 18 holes of golf. In this way, those golfers who have less natural talent than others are able to compete on a more equitable basis.

Many white Americans cry foul against affirmative action, arguing that this amounts to unfair reverse discrimination. To assign people automatic credit just because they are black in cases of gaining aid or entrance to college, or for a job opening, is to ignore merit and to penalize individual whites by suppressing their ability to fairly compete with blacks. Racial discrimination, they plead, is unfair, and two wrongs do not make a right.

Perhaps the above argument strikes "the bottom line" on this issue. The use of Affirmative Action schemes may be an unjust response to another injustice–hence unwarranted. On the other hand, this issue may be too vague and complex to decide. Yet if we ask ourselves, "Which is the greater injustice?", we may also conclude that what we have here is a case of the "chickens coming home to roost." If we assume that injustice should be corrected and that blacks have been placed in a most disadvantaged and undeserved position in our society due to white racism–the moral imperative is to correct this injustice. It is hard to see how this injustice can be compensated for in any reasonable amount of time unless we resort to devices like Affirmative Action. If injustice is involved both in the second class-status of blacks and in the most reasonable means of remedying this injustice, the right conclusion may be that we should seek to eliminate the greater of the two injustices.

Blacks in America have been brutalized or unfairly discriminated against for three or four hundred years. The humiliating and demoralizing effects of this discrimination continue to malinger in our society. As a result, we may point out two facts. One, a severe injustice was done to all American blacks through slavery and the denial of civil rights until the middle of this century. These injustices done to blacks in the past ought to be corrected. Two, most blacks today are at a disadvantage in competing with whites due to the debilitating effects of those severe injustices of the past. There ought to be compensation for blacks being disadvantaged in this way.

With regard to the first point, whites may be tempted to take a "water under the bridge" attitude. Thus, some may argue that these severe injustices done in the past *to blacks who no longer exist* cannot be corrected, since those victimized are dead, as are those people whose practices victimized them. We have no relevant way to correct such past injustice. This argument is convenient for whites who want to wash their hands of the past and their connectedness to the past, but the reasoning is not decisive. Our concerns outlive us, as is illustrated by life insurance policies, wills, and the struggles to make life better for our children and their children. Most of us have hopes and desires for the welfare of family, friends, our nation or culture which transcend our brief existence on earth. A promise to a person is not nullified merely because the person no longer exists. Such facts have long been acknowledged by the law, and no reason exists to exclude morality from this "territory."

Who would those blacks who were brutalized by past slavery, murder, beatings, and denial of civil rights, want to benefit from compensatory justice? The most reasonable answer is: their descendants and other blacks. Therefore, to correct the more severe injustices done to blacks by white racism in the past, we should compensate today's black citizens. This brings us to the second fact–the disadvantaged competitive position of most blacks today due to the effects of past discriminatory practices. If we are to compensate for the severe past injustices done to blacks by compensating today's blacks, and if today's blacks are competitively handicapped by the legacy of white racism, the most relevant remedy would be to turn their traditional handicap (their skin color) into a benefit. In other words, when competing with whites for jobs or educational opportunities, allow their blackness to count as a mark in their favor (rather than as the "mark of Cain"). To treat their blackness neutrally in this regard–given the disadvantage it has caused them–would amount to resolving to stop further penalizing blacks rather than compensating them for the handicap with which they have been unjustly burdened. If you have been drowning people, justice does not require merely that you stop pushing them down, it requires that you pull them above water (and, if need be, administer artificial respiration).

Individual white folks can plead their innocence of such racist treatment of blacks, but American society, institutions, and laws cannot easily be divorced from liability and responsibility for compensatory justice. Slavery and other denials of the civil rights of blacks have been institutionally sanctioned by our society, and it is thus relevant for compensation to be rendered blacks by the institutional mechanisms of society. In any event, we need not treat our society as a person (metaphorically) in order to argue this point. A plausible moral principle is that injustice is to be corrected insofar as it is known and possible to do so. Under this rubric, our society's immense institutional power gives us (as individuals) the ability to correct the racist injustices done to our black citizens.

Finally, we must compare the racist injustices done to blacks with the unfairness done to individual whites who may–if Affirmative Action is applied–fail to gain financial aids for education or fail to be hired for jobs due to the compensatory special treatment afforded black Americans. Given the severity of past racism against blacks and the continuing handicapping effects of such racism, I do not see how the unfairness done to some white folks could be construed as anywhere near the severity of injustices done to blacks by racism in our society. This conclusion is only heightened when I consider that the financial and moral "support networks" available to whites in our country are much more accessible and extensive than those open to blacks.

The purist may argue that we have no reason to choose between the lesser of two injustices here because it is never right to address one injustice by causing innocent parties to suffer. It is wrong to try to correct injustice by causing injustice. I can only reply that this is not plausible or realistic. Whenever anyone who is guilty of a serious crime is correctly convicted and sentenced to jail (even supposing that our prisons were, what many are not, civilized institutions of confinement and correction), they have friends and loved ones who suffer, and who do not deserve such suffering. As long as injustice exists in our world, both the guilty and the innocent will in some measure suffer the consequences of that injustice. The only realistic way of alleviating this sad fact is to strive, insofar as we can, first to eliminate the sources of great injustice. Denying our responsibility for alleviating injustice by whimpering that we are wholly innocent or by arguing that there can be no justice without perfect (pure) justice, is the surest way to further the problem rather than the solution. It is childish.

The issue is emotionally rousing and complex. It reminds us of cases of legitimate, competing claims on justice and the ethical necessity of trying to be as fair as possible in adjudicating such claims.

Granting that some moral issues can be horribly complex and ambiguous, the mistake would be to infer that if a moral issue appears incapable of a definite right or wrong answer, the issue must be purely subjective. That the issue appears so, even after persistent, valiant efforts to resolve it, does not mean that it is incapable of a right or wrong answer. The issue may involve great complexities; many facts and values may need to be sorted out and balanced. Even purely factual questions can involve great ambiguity and be so complex as to defy conscientious efforts to arrive at a definite answer. The workings of state economies often are a case in point. Questions arise concerning the cause of inflation, unemployment, and lower productivity, and the answers depend upon so many factors that accurate predictions and explanations may be virtually impossible. Even the most self-assured, economic pundits are occasionally stupefied at turns in economic events. Weather forecasting is another case in point. A meteorologist may have an enormous amount of past and present weather data available, yet be unsure whether a low pressure area will move (and at what pace) to the north, northeast, or east. Consequently, the meteorologist may be uncertain whether it is likely to rain in central Missouri tomorrow.

Ambiguity and difficulty are not unique to moral issues, and human biases and emotions can make moral issues appear fuzzier than they are. Lack of education, impatience, anger, desire for revenge, spite, and laziness can influence our considerations, making a decision about right and wrong more ambiguous than it should be. The greatest complicating subjective factor is our desire to think well of ourselves. Most of us are strongly inclined to believe that we are basically good or sensitive people. Oh, we may make an occasional blunder, but overall our intentions and actions are good. So we think. The more we can view a situation as tremendously vague, ambiguous, or complicated–the more we shift responsibility for our action (or inaction) away from ourselves. The fuzzier the world which calls upon us for a decision, the less we can be blamed for whatever we decide. Since most of us fear being blamed more than we long to be praised for our actions, we become good at rationalizing. We learn how to magnify the complexity and ambiguity of the world in order to minimize our responsibility for deciding. For some, the occasional defense of moral relativism or subjectivism is essential to rationalizing their behavior, to making it more bearable to live with themselves.

Finally, why should we assume that moral vagueness or ambiguity implies that morality is a subjective affair? Must reality be definite or clear-cut if it is objective reality? It is hard to see why it must be, hence hard to see why moral reality must be definite or clear-cut. Consider the observable world. Fuzziness occurs in the color of things in the world. We cannot always say what is black and what is white, blue vs. green, or red vs. orange. Not only does gray occur between black and white, but sometimes we cannot decide whether a color is black or gray, or gray or white. Is this vagueness subjective? Why should we think so? This same fuzziness can be found among sounds, tastes, feels, and smells. Even scientists are now accustomed to accepting indefiniteness as an integral part of the world. Physicists are willing to speak of light in terms not of waves or particles, but wavicles. Quantum physicists speak not in terms of the cause of an event, but merely of its probability of occurrence. Causation may not always be a matter of one event making another event inevitable, but of an event making another likely to occur.

We are used to thinking of the definite as a sign of objectivity and the indefinite as a sign of subjectivity–but our minds' desire for the definite may stand truth on its head. Perhaps the indefinite characterizes the objective, while the definite characterizes the subjective. Even this way of speaking is an oversimplified falsification. It is not the objective which is characterized by the indefinite–but reality. It is not the subjective (which is, after all, a part of reality) which is characterized by the definite, but our minds' desire for rationality. That is, a part of us demands, both subconsciously and consciously, that reality be lucid and definite. We see planets as spherical and their orbits as circular, but the truth is not so ideal. Planets are egg-shaped, and their orbits are elliptical. We see patterns in the clouds and the heavens–patterns which we have only recently realized are arbitrary impositions. The real truth is that reality, both objective and subjective, is rich enough to admit the definite and the indefinite. The longing for what is definite is an offshoot of the subjective, of our desire to make sense out of this "buzzing, blooming confusion."

If this much is granted, then we should expect that some moral questions will appear fuzzy, and that some are–by their very nature–indeterminate. For some moral issues–perhaps abortion–rightness and wrongness may be impossible to decisively determine.

4. Moral "Fact": Who Is to Judge?

Let us now examine the question of who decides what is right and wrong. As I have argued, it is an error to answer that God decides–unless you mean that God would be in the best position (being infinitely wise) to discern infallibly what is right and what is wrong. The question here concerns we fallible human beings and how we are to decide right and wrong.

As Kierkegaard and Sartre were keenly aware, we cannot delegate our moral decisions to God. Kierkegaard was a Danish, Christian philosopher of the nineteenth century whose thought was significant in the twentieth-century development of Christian existentialism. The French philosopher Jean-Paul Sartre was mainly responsible for the development in this century of atheistic existentialism. Two central values of existentialism are honesty and the value of subjectivity. Existentialism stresses the importance of accepting personal responsibility for our values and actions. We cannot delegate our moral responsibility in the narrow sense that we cannot blame God for our decision to kill. Furthermore, following God's will is no substitute for following our conscience. As soon as we can say that a "value" is some authority's edict or legislation, we can reduce our personal responsibility for accepting or rejecting that value. You can hear bureaucrats and police say, "I don't make the laws, I just enforce them." In a similar fashion, a soldier or citizen can rationalize the mechanical and passive acceptance of regulations. We become so good at this buck-passing that eventually the responsibility for decisions is diffused to the vanishing point. People are not responsible, the System is. Whatever justification may sometimes exist for such rationalizations, we deceive ourselves if we imagine that being moral is simply a matter of following God's regulations.

Consider the story of Abraham and Isaac. One evening a voice spoke to Abraham commanding him to kill his son Isaac as a sacrifice to God. Abraham had a terrible decision to make. Should he have faith in this voice and commit what we consider to be one of the worst forms of murder, or should he refrain from killing his beloved son and risk the wrath of an angry God? Who was to decide? Abraham, of course. But could he have made his decision simply by placing his faith in the Will of God? No. That route was a dead-end for several reasons. First, it was at least possible that there was no God. Second, and more importantly, if God existed, there would remain the need for interpreting God's will. Let us put ourselves in Abraham's place (and thank our lucky stars that we are not really in his place). What is God's will here? We cannot answer simply that God has decreed the sacrifice of Isaac. Was this God's voice? Might it not have been a hideous nightmare, or a temptation from Satan, or a sign that Abraham was insane? At Abraham's advanced age (he was over 100 by that time), senility could not be ruled out. Even if Abraham were by now accustomed to the distinctive voice of God, having been spoken to before by the Lord, such doubts would be reasonable. Who, for example, could prove to Abraham that Satan was not capable of impersonating God's voice in order to lead people astray? And who was more likely to command a father to "murder" his son? It was certainly not, as Abraham was well-aware, God's will, in general, for people to kill one another, much less for a father to slay his innocent son. Further, God had promised Abraham that Isaac's seed would be blessed and that he would be the father of many nations. How could this be true if young Isaac was slain? Surely, therefore, this awful command must not be from God. On the other hand, who are we to judge the Infallible? God might expect awful tests of our faith. Was this a test? We know that it had a happy ending (since God offered a lamb as a substitute sacrifice at the last moment). Poor Abraham did not. He had to decide without such comfort.

Abraham could not delegate his responsibility for deciding what was right to the regulations of God. The passages in holy scripture would not have helped him. He was on his own, left to decide for himself what was God's will. In a similar way, so are all of us on our own in the moral arena. Even if a perfectly moral Being exists, it is still up to us to figure out what is right and what is wrong. This is unsettling.

It would be so much easier, so much more comforting if it were just a matter of following the commands of divine authority. Consider the rules of a private firm or government agency. No matter how silly, unfathomable, or absurd the rules seem to be, employees can take some comfort in knowing they are not responsible for the decisions which instituted those rules. Yet in the moral arena, we cannot escape personal responsibility by following the commands of authority. We must decide for ourselves, even if this amounts only to the unreflective choice to follow the authority's orders. True, our decisions do not literally make something right or wrong; our authority does not extend that far. Still, no one else can decide for us what is right and wrong; this responsibility rests squarely on each of our shoulders.

A further complication makes our situation unsettling. Most of us dislike being criticized, and many of us go to great lengths to shelter ourselves from the possibility of criticism. We may be infatuated with the thought of unchallenged authority. Think of an authority where, by reason of great power or insight, no reproach is possible. You may hear slogans like: "As long as I am paying the bills, you will live by my rules." Individuals and nations learn to settle disputes by beating, or threatening to beat, the other into submission. Yet if each of us must decide what is right and wrong and if we are all liable to make some mistakes in moral judgment, we are not entitled to a position of unchallenged authority. It is not as though we are perfect decision-makers who have invented the game of morality. We are quite imperfect, we did not create the game, yet we must play it. We cannot escape the scrutiny of others. Each of us is–in a real sense–our brothers' and sisters' keeper.

When people ask rhetorically, "Who decides what's right and wrong?", they express a fear and make several misguided assumptions. They may fear moral imperialism and authoritarianism; they fear that someone will be set up as the arbitrary dictator of morality for everyone. Fearing moral imperialism or authoritarianism is legitimate, but we need not construe morality as wholly emotional or subjective in order to avoid these evils. If no elite decides what is right and wrong (or if we all "decide" this, as I think is the case), then the main concern which underlies, "Who decides?" vanishes. Another fear may be present–a fear that moral issues will prove objective and difficult, requiring strenuous effort to resolve. We may fear having to expose our convictions to others' inspection when they contradict ours. Such a fear may not only indicate a person's fear of being vulnerable, it may indicate laziness. In wondering who is to decide moral questions, a person may also assume that, contrary to factual matters, we cannot perceive right and wrong, good and evil, justice and injustice. If we could, then just as we can perceive black and white, we could easily resolve moral questions. In other words, it wouldn't be so much a matter of "deciding" right and wrong as a matter of observing the facts.

Is it true that we cannot perceive right and wrong, good and evil? Surely, we can perceive thefts, lies, and murders. Yet the first two are normally examples of wrong, and murder is always wrong. Doesn't this mean that we *can* perceive right and wrong? No, our skeptic will argue, because we are unable to identify what we observe in these acts which makes the act wrong. We can point out what feature we observe that leads us to call an object black versus white: there is a color to point to. But this is not so in the case of right and wrong. We may point to an act as wrong, yet aside from its other perceivable features, we cannot point out what quality we perceive that makes it wrong.

The feeling that moral values are imperceivable and ultimately subjective is a deep-rooted suspicion. Whether we can perceive right and wrong is a question which raises other fundamental questions. To have genuine moral knowledge, must it be gained through perception? If not, how else could we gain knowledge of right and wrong?

In this chapter, I have argued against a number of misconceptions about morality. I have argued that in an important sense we are misguided to ask who "decides" what is right and wrong. Before discussing my theory of moral right and wrong, another misconception about morality deserves examination. This is the view that morally unselfish action is somehow impossible for us. I shall examine this view in Chapter Three.

Three

HOW SELF-CENTERED SHOULD WE BE?

Human selfishness remains a favorite topic of everyday discussion. Pronouncements and disputes about it are endless. It is almost inconceivable that someone could go through life without being criticized occasionally for being selfish. A fact of human existence is that we criticize one another, and even ourselves, for acting selfishly. Selfish behavior has from generation to generation received nearly universal bad press. From a traditional moral view, it is no exaggeration to say that all moral vices can be construed as effects (or particular forms) of human selfishness. Certainly this has been the focus within the Christian tradition. Consider the Commandment, "Love Thy Neighbor As Thyself." Even though our naturally sinful condition inclines us to act selfishly (and we can be expected to often behave selfishly), our traditional ethic insists we can and should act unselfishly.

Yet many thinkers have viewed selfishness otherwise. In ancient Greece, Plato discussed the view[1] of some (though he rejected it) that justice is nothing but the interests of the stronger or ruling party. The many–who are weaker–are naturally prepared to reject such an understanding of justice. One century ago, the philosopher Nietzsche endorsed a similar view by arguing that the will to power[2] (as opposed to truth or justice) is our primary motivation. He ridiculed the morality of pity and unselfishness as a deception which could well lead to individual and cultural suicide. In this century, renewed pleas have emerged for a revaluation of the concept of selfishness. In the name of honesty, prudence, and mental health, authors have argued for the virtues of selfishness and even for the impossibility of our acting unselfishly. Popular books like *Looking Out for Number One*[3], *How I Found Freedom in an Unfree World*,[4] and *The Virtue of Selfishness*,[5] have told us that we should "do our own thing" if only because ultimately this is all we can do.

In democracies, especially in capitalist democracies, a tendency exists to extol the virtues of selfishness. Such societies hold sacred the value of freedom, the rights of the individual, and the right of private profit. Here we should not be surprised if the value of unfettered self-expression is placed on a pedestal. Our ancestors were taught that acting selfishly is wrong, but we moderns have been invited to rethink the ancient dogma. While we still suspect that selfish behavior is wrong, we also wonder whether our suspicion is neurotic. Perhaps our negative attitude toward selfishness is a lingering habit, the unquestioned reflex of millennia of cultural conditioning. Increasingly, people wonder whether talk about guilt over such behavior is just the "g-word", full of sound and fury, but signifying nothing healthy. Increasingly, we long to be freed from the bonds of ancient superstitions.

In what follows, I offer both good news and bad news for modern folks. The good news is twofold. First, it is healthy and right for us to be "self-centered," provided this is understood properly. Likewise, it is unhealthy and wrong for us to think we must act in such a way that we think only of others. Second, I offer good news to those moderns who feel beleaguered by the "enlightened" view which praises selfishness and damns the very coherency of the concept of unselfish behavior. For those who feel besieged by the ideology of self-gratification, I will support their conviction that something is fundamentally wrong with such thinking. The so-called "enlightened" view of rational egoism represents not progress, but confusion. Such good news is, also bad news for modern egoists. I also have bad news for those who yearn to believe that all feelings of guilt are inherently irrational. It still makes sense for us to feel bad about our having acted selfishly. It still is sensible for us to think that we can do too much for ourselves. My aim is to reveal and explode some egoistic myths. I mean to show that acting "selfishly" is, after all, a moral evil to be minimized if not eliminated.

1. What Is Selfish Behavior?

Leave it to a philosopher to raise such a question. Isn't it clear what selfishness is? I think not. Some thinkers argue we ought to act selfishly, because we human beings are incapable of acting unselfishly. By their recommendation to act "selfishly," they mean that each of us ought to do what is in our self-interest, and that when others' interests conflict with ours, we are not obliged to defer to them unless we freely choose to do so. Let us call this view "egoism" of a kind. In philosophy we distinguish between normative egoism (we ought to behave selfishly) and psychological egoism (we always behave with a selfish motivation). Debate continues about how "egoism" should be defined.[6] Egoists believe that each of us is and ought to be self-centered–the many centers of the moral universe. They believe that rationality implies that no value standard exists–not community, the welfare of others, or God's will–which should have priority over doing what is in the self-interest of each of us. They also think that selfish action *is* doing what we think will please us or doing things in order to please ourselves. They are wrong about this.

Consider their rationale. Here are some examples of what we normally think of as selfish actions:

1. Juan refuses to share any of his candy with his little sister, who has no candy of her own.

2. For their anniversary, which is very meaningful to his wife, Chad buys tickets to a Royals' baseball game, even though he knows she has no interest in baseball.

3. Patricia expects her lover to pay attention to her when she talks about her job as a teacher, but pays little attention to him when he discusses his work.

4. Al, a small family farmer needs continued access to the water controlled legally by the large farm owned by the Exxon Corporation. Without it, Al's farm and family will not survive. Exxon's executives refuse Al continued access to the water because he cannot pay the price they are asking for it, and because they would like to buy Al's land to add to their acreage.

We can easily spot the selfishness in such cases, but giving an exact account of the nature of what we've spotted is not easy. The egoist will likely say that what we spot in such cases are people doing things because it pleases them to do so. In other words, whenever people act, they do so in order to avoid pain or to attain pleasure. Little Juan is pleased to keep all of his candy to himself, Chad is pleased to go to a baseball game, Patricia is pleased to be needed, etc. These people act as they do because it pleases them. That's part of human nature: we always act in order to please ourselves, we always act selfishly.

But a critic might ask, what about the following sorts of cases?

5. Boris despises family gatherings, but attends this one because he feels it is his duty.

6. Kim Sung throws himself on a live grenade in order to save the lives of his fellow soldiers.

7. Carmelita burns herself alive to protest U.S. military involvement in El Salvador.

Don't these cases show that people are willing to do very unpleasant things, things they would much rather not do? Aren't these cases where the motive is duty, not pleasure or pain?

2. Can We Act Unselfishly?

No, the egoist will say to the above questions. First of all, a difference exists between doing something which is inherently pleasing to us and doing something which has pleasing consequences. Boris may not enjoy attending family gatherings, but he may enjoy acting according to what he feels is his duty. Second, a big difference exists between it pleasing us to perform an action and our receiving pleasure from performing it. Boris may not derive pleasure from attending the gathering, but he does so in order to avoid the guilt he will otherwise feel–it pleases him because he avoids pain. Third, people often do things they would rather not do in order to attain or avoid something else. Carmelita would rather not burn herself alive, but she may do so because she would rather do this than ignore her conscience.[7] Thus, people do things they would rather not do, but only where it pleases them more than doing otherwise. We always mean to do what we are pleased most to do.[8] Finally, the egoist will argue that neither Boris, Kim Sung, nor Carmelita act *due to duty* rather than pleasure or pain. Boris' action will be interpreted as done in order to avoid guilt or obtain the satisfaction of doing his duty. Kim Sung's act may be interpreted as done because it pleases him to act heroically. Carmelita's gruesome act will be interpreted as done in order to satisfy her conscience.

Egoists appear to have a strong case, since they can easily show how all of our actions are "selfish." But appearances are sometimes deceiving, and this is a case in point. Their view is simple to comprehend, simple to apply, and apparently powerful because it allows us to explain all human behavior. Nevertheless, simplicity can be a vice, and something can be quite powerful yet misguided.

3. My View of Selfishness

The egoist assumes that selfish behavior is behavior performed because it pleases us. Is this true? Suppose I am at home on a weekend by myself, and I decide to watch a baseball game on TV. I do this because I think I will enjoy watching the game. Is my act, therefore, selfish? It doesn't seem so. Suppose my friend enters the room and says: "Oh, being selfish again, ay? Doing something because it pleases you?" This would be odd. We never criticize someone or get criticized for being selfish just because we are doing something we enjoy.

When do we get criticized for acting selfishly? This occurs when we do something at someone else's expense. Being selfish is being inconsiderate of others, and being inconsiderate is to ignore or violate the legitimate needs and interests of others. If I want something badly and you have little interest in it, but you take it because you feel like it at the time–we would call your act selfish in the moral sense of "selfish." If a young child needs mother's affection and the mother gives it only sporadically because "she has her own life to lead," we would say that the mother is selfish. If one adult desperately needs some tenderness from another adult and the other refuses to give it because it is an inconvenience, we might call such a refusal selfish. If one nation squanders most of the world's energy resources at the expense of many more needy countries, we might well call such squandering selfish.

Not all needs and interests are "legitimate," which means that we are not morally required to cater to just any desire or whim of others. For example, if Harry hates the way long hair looks on men, other men are not acting inconsiderately of Harry by wearing long hair. For human beings to be happy and to have any dignity at all, they must be allowed "their own space," an area in life in which they may do as they please without the interference of busybodies. Harry's attitude here represents busybody interference if he insists that others comply with it. Consider some more examples. If one person demands that another spend all of her time with him, even though such a possessive relationship would make the other quite unhappy, the demand is not legitimate; indeed, it is selfish. If a thief wants all of your money, you are not being inconsiderate by resisting the thief. If someone needs your help to oppress or torture others, you are not being inconsiderate to refuse assistance. In general, the difference between legitimate and illegitimate needs and interests has to do with (1) whether the person merely wants or really needs the thing in question, (2) whose needs are the greater, (3) who is more deserving, (4) whether the need or want can be frustrated without serious harm being done, and (5) whether the need or want is healthy or not.

If I am right about the morally relevant meaning of "selfish," this shows that the egoist theory of human motivation is misguided. This indicates we are capable of unselfish acts. Each of us do little things every day (perhaps in private) which seldom if ever conflict with the legitimate needs and interests of others. Consider how strange it would normally be to label the following as selfish: brushing our teeth, drinking a glass of water, twiddling our thumbs, scratching our arm, skipping as we walk to work, having a coffee during our morning break, and so on. We do many things because it pleases us to do so, yet such actions are not selfish. If so, then from a moral point of view, the egoist gets off on the wrong foot by presuming that selfish acts equal acts which please us or which are done because they please us. Simplicity is not a virtue when it consists in error.

I propose that selfish behavior amounts to our acting inconsiderately of others. All our intentional actions reflect our self-concern. To be alive, awake, and meaning to do something, always implies a level of concern for ourselves. For example, acting out of conscience is acting out of concern for what we believe to be right or honorable, and our personal values are part of what defines our self-identity. Nevertheless, while acting out of conscience implies self-concerned action, it is ridiculous to think such action is selfish. All of our intentional actions are self-concerned actions, but what makes them selfish is whether we show too much concern for ourselves and too little for others. As Aristotle noted long ago, balanced behavior is morally required. Just as we can show too much concern for ourselves, so too can we show too little concern for ourselves. When we show too little concern for ourselves, we act in a self-neglectful or abusive manner. Such action is *not* unselfish, hence, morally praiseworthy; it is self-destructive. From a moral point of view, each of us is of equal worth. It is, therefore, morally wrong to think that your needs and desires are inherently less important than those of others. Unselfish behavior is not utterly self-less or self-sacrificing behavior (which is pathological and born of low self-esteem), but action which exhibits a proper balancing of your interests and the interests of others. This means that an action may be "self-centered" yet unselfish.

Consider the example of Jesus. No one more clearly illustrates the commitment to caring for others. Was Jesus a person who had no concern for himself? A person with low self-esteem? A masochist bent on self-destructive behavior? Some will think this is the most natural way to interpret him–but are we compelled to think of Jesus as a weak-willed or suicidal personality? I think not. Suppose we consider Jesus divine. If so, we can hardly think of his behavior as symptomatic of a poorly developed ego. How can God have low self-esteem or weak will? How can God be self-destructive? No, we must admit that all egos pale in comparison to the Divine. Suppose, on the other hand that Jesus was merely human, albeit a most unusual, a most remarkable human being. His unique behavior lets us know that we cannot expect to explain his motivation in exactly the same way we would explain typical human behavior. I suppose that nothing here rules out the following profile of Jesus' motives. Imagine a person so sensitive to the suffering of others that he was barely able to notice his own suffering. Better yet, imagine a person whose greatest suffering was aroused precisely by his perception of the agony of others. Imagine that he was most affected by the suffering of the powerless, the poor, the afflicted, and the pitiful. A person whose deepest desire was to heal this massive pain, and who fervently believed that compassion required us to forswear all violence as a means to our ends. Wouldn't such a person be tormented by the pitiful abyss between his ideals and the human reality he confronted? Wouldn't he prefer misunderstanding and crucifixion to doing anything which would betray his ideals?

I am not arguing that this is the only coherent portrait possible for Jesus, but I do argue it is coherent, possible, and plausible. Hence, we can suppose Jesus to have been one of the most powerful egos (one of the most "self-centered") ever to have existed. His will-power was immense. We find no traces of cowardice or anemia here. Was he self-destructive? Only if we assume that clinging to earthly life is the only, or the most important, way to protect our sense of self. Even if most of us would say "yes" to this, this hardly means that exceptional people must be motivated by the same hierarchy of values. Still, can't we say safely that Jesus neglected his interests, that he showed an extremely unbalanced concern for others? I think not. What were Jesus' interests? Do we have evidence he ever regretted the choices which brought him an early death? We must first take such questions seriously before we can "safely" pronounce Jesus to have abused his best interests. So long as it remains conceivable that an individual could exist (rare to be sure) who is capable of such ideals and such compassion, we cannot judge this behavior on the same scale we apply to ordinary mortals. Given such values and such intense compassion, we should be surprised if this behavior was less other-directed than it was.

Thus, I imagine Jesus' profound concern for others to have been a direct expression of his profound fidelity to his own values. This is the sign of great self-concern. Because Jesus loved himself so much, he was able to express such love for others. This explains why Jesus could recommend "Love Thy Neighbor As Thy Self" as one of the two highest Commandments.[9] Unless we assume that an unstated part of the meaning here is "Love Thy Self," this Commandment sanctions treating our neighbor poorly if we poorly love ourself. In any case, we can say that self-love does not imply selfishness.

Suppose I am right that a continuum exists of possible self-concern such that excessive self-concern is selfishness and deficient self-concern is self-abuse. How then do we determine what is "excessive"*versus* "deficient" self-concern? Some readers may think my interpretation of Jesus raises this question. What criteria do we have for making such judgments?

Our self-interest involves our needs and desires. So long as our needs and desires are healthy, so long as it would be healthy for us to satisfy them, they should be satisfied. Beyond this, a hierarchy should be considered. Our needs are more vital than our desires because our physical and emotional well-being is more broadly and deeply dependent upon getting what we need than on getting what we want. You would hardly take pleasure in simple amusements if you are starving to death. It is likewise difficult to enjoy what you normally enjoy when you feel unloved (say, because your beloved died). Finally, survival needs take precedence over other needs; being properly fed is more vital than finding social acceptance. This is true for the same reason that needs are more vital than desires. Assuming then that each of our self-interests are equally valuable, we can turn to the above criteria to decide whether we are being excessively, deficiently, or appropriately self-concerned.

Consider example 3. We can assume that both Patricia and her lover desire to be paid attention to when they speak. Since there is no question here (we may suppose) of a need outweighing a desire, both of their desires deserve to be satisfied. Since Patricia is concerned about her desire being fulfilled, but shows no concern for fulfilling her lover's co-equal desire–she acts out of excessive self-concern (and operates with a double-standard).

Consider example 4. Al needs access to the water supply for survival, while Exxon's desire here is not corporate survival, but expansion and greed. Consequently, Al's actions to gain access to the water are those of appropriate self-concern. Exxon's self-interests here are not co-equal with Al's because Exxon's desires are less vital. Therefore, Exxon would be showing an excessive self-concern–selfishness.

Recall example 1. Both Juan and his sister desire the candy; neither needs the candy (we may suppose). Even if Juan bought the candy or was given it as a gift, we may suppose that both of their desires could be satisfied if Juan shared some of his candy with his sister. Since their desires are co-equal, Juan could satisfy both of their desires, yet he concerns himself only with his desire. He acts selfishly. He shows an unbalanced concern for himself.

Finally, consider example 2. Chad plans for he and his wife to attend a baseball game on their anniversary. His wife dislikes baseball and does take seriously the symbolism of celebrating their anniversary. If she passively consents to Chad's plan and does not assert herself in an effort to achieve a compromise with her husband, she is showing an unbalanced concern for Chad. She is abusing herself. Chad may be acting both selfishly and self-abusively. Their desires for how to have fun are co-equal, yet here those desires conflict with one another. By acting as if his desire was more important, especially when a compromise outing might prove satisfying to both, Chad acts selfishly. Furthermore, their anniversary celebration is a symbol of commitment to their relationship. If Chad glosses over the emotional symbolism of how they spend this special day, he may well be weakening a bond which he needs. Since our needs outweigh our desires, he would be abusing his self-interest by focusing on short-term amusement rather than long-term emotional needs.

I do not intend by this discussion to specify criteria for selfish, unselfish, or self-abusive behavior which will allow us always to decide without doubt who acts selfishly and who does not. Our concept of selfishness is not that precise, but it is precise enough to indicate that selfishness *versus* unselfishness is not divided by the presence or absence of self-concern. What matters is how we express our self-concern in terms of the following principles:

(1) Each person's needs or desires (unless unhealthy) are co-equal in importance with any other person's needs or desires.

(2) Healthy needs or desires are more important than unhealthy needs or desires.

(3) Needs are more important than desires.

(4) Some kinds of needs are more important than other kinds of needs.

I have not discussed the nature of the "healthy" *versus* "unhealthy," and the application of these concepts can often be fraught with disagreement and controversy. Nevertheless, this distinction is normally clear enough to virtually all of us. Self-destructive desires are not healthy. Compulsive, obsessive, and self-damaging needs are not healthy. A desire for perfection is unhealthy for imperfect creatures. The need of alcoholics for drinking is unhealthy. The desire of nicotine addicts to smoke cigarettes is not healthy. On the other hand, the desire to eat supper is healthy. The need for love is healthy. The need to protect yourself is healthy.

4. A Critique of the Egoists' Theory of Motivation

Even if egoists are misguided about our concept of selfishness, are they nevertheless right that we do everything in order to please ourselves? Are they right on target in suggesting that we always do what we think–given the circumstances–would *most* please us? Have they hit on the underlying principle of human motivation? I don't think so. In any event, we have reason to doubt their story.

According to their account, whenever we do something, we do it in order to avoid pain or gain pleasure. This could involve a process of deliberation or calculation, or it could amount to a quasi-mechanistic view that we automatically tend to do what will please us. Even in cases of spontaneous or impulsive action and in cases where we think that a person's motive is the well-being of others, the person's underlying motive is self-satisfaction. Why did the father dash into the burning building? To save his infant daughter? No, according to the egoist view. Oh, this ordinary explanation can suffice as a superficial account, but the underlying motive (of which we are often not conscious) was his desire to avoid the agony to himself if his daughter perished. Why did the "altruist" give so much of her time and money to helping AIDS victims? Out of concern for their suffering? No. The deeper explanation lies in the pleasure it gave her to help others or in her desire to avoid the guilt she feels when she does not follow her conscience.

Why are such explanations "deeper" than our ordinary ones? Well, we need to ask why the father preferred to save his child, why the "altruist" prefers to help those who suffer. Once we raise these questions, we see that the general form of our answer will point to the person's likes and dislikes. By doing so, we gain a general theory for predicting what people will do: they seek to avoid pain and to gain pleasure. Consider Skinner's behaviorist theory of operant conditioning.[10] Behavior which is positively reinforced will tend to be repeated. Behavior which is negatively reinforced will tend to disappear. What in particular pleases people (due to a positive reinforcer) or displeases people (due to a negative reinforcer) varies greatly. Still, a common denominator exists. All of us seek to avoid negative reinforcers and to approach positive reinforcers.

In spite of the surface appeal of this "deeper" account, which resembles common sense and folk psychology, it is doubtful that it provides a more accurate alternative to our ordinary explanations of human behavior. For one matter, we can ask why something pleases or displeases a person. For example, why does it displease the father that his infant daughter might die? Presumably, the explanation will have something to do with the biological and cultural history of the father. Does this mean that this "third-level" explanation is deeper and more accurate? If so, what about the "fourth-level" explanation of why those biological and cultural facts existed as they did? There will be an indefinite series of "motivational" explanations, each successive one making the prior one shallow and inaccurate by comparison. This approach is, in practice, absurd. We would have to reject as shallow any explanation of why a person acts which does not lead us back at least as far as the alleged cosmic Big Bang (or to God). We would be better off to say the father dashed into the burning building to save his child. It is accurate, and it spares us from the kind of quest for "prior" explanations which we can never complete.

Another problem arises here. Granting that often we do things to gain pleasure or avoid pain, and granted that receiving pleasure or not receiving pain are typical consequences of our actions, what is the justification for maintaining that these are always the motives of our behavior? Consequences or effects of our actions are not necessarily our goals or motives. Our actions have many effects, not just pain or pleasure, and we cannot validly infer that because an effect typically results from our intentional behavior, our motive for so-acting is that effect.

Let us not oversimplify human existence. Consider some examples which bring out the nature of three possible consequences of our actions: pain, pleasure, and a neutral state intermediate between pain and pleasure. If I burn my hand, I receive pain. If I am insulted by a loved one, I receive pain (hurt, anxiety). If I am abandoned by a friend or lover, I feel pain (hurt, anxiety). On the other hand, eating fudge sundaes, having sex, or listening to my favorite music may bring me pleasure. Still, many habitual things I do, do not really bring me pleasure or pain (although being prevented from doing them might well cause me pain). Most of the walking and individual steps I take every day, in my home or at work–produce neither pleasure nor pain. (Of course, if I have a bad leg, such walking might have far different effects on me). Most of the little half-conscious gestures we make day-in and day-out bring us neither pleasure nor pain (unless we become self-conscious of them). Think of the times you've done something quite ordinary like reaching for the hot water faucet on your kitchen sink. How often did doing that produce pleasure or pain? Compare this with the pleasure you get from your favorite foods, drinks, games, drugs, sexual acts, and friends. Think also of the pain of broken bones, burns, slaps, punches, diseases, toothaches, and heartaches. Isn't it strained to force a sensation of pleasure or pain into such an ordinary circumstance? So it seems to me. True, we can understandably say that it "pleased us" to reach for the faucet–but this fact can be quite different from our doing so in order to receive a sensation of pleasure. Likewise, even if we receive no sensation of pleasure from not being in pain, it "pleases us" not to be in pain.

So the egoists have noticed that our actions are typically, if not universally, accompanied by pleasure or pain. From this, they may infer that the reason we do things is to gain pleasure or avoid pain. They are the victims of one greatly mistaken assumption: if pain and pleasure are usually or always effects of what we do intentionally, pain or pleasure must be the goals of what we do. Effects and goals are not the same. All actualized goals are effects, but not all effects are goals. Let us make this more concrete. Whenever we do anything, we push air molecules about. Does this mean that the great, underlying purpose (goal) of all behavior is to push air molecules about? Hardly. Effects, even if universally produced by us, are not, therefore, human goals. In this case, we might better say that this effect is an unavoidable side-effect of our doing anything at all.

Consider this too. When we eat or drink something, we swallow it. Does this mean that our true motive in eating or drinking is to swallow? Of course not. Consider another example. Whenever we do anything (whether awake or asleep, dead or alive) we either bump into a rhinoceros or we do not. Does this mean the ultimate goal of all human action is to bump into or avoid bumping into a rhinoceros? Again, this is absurd.

But the egoist may complain that my examples are unfair. We normally are not aware that we push air molecules around, normally we are barely aware (if at all) of swallowing our food or drink, and we certainly do not consider possible confrontations with rhinos. Yet we are all quite aware, and from an early age, of the attractive power of pleasure and the unattractive power of pain. We also realize, from an early age, that we can gain pleasure and avoid pain by what we do. Hence, it is plausible to imagine our naturally being prone to do what will bring us the one and help us avoid the other.

One of the egoist's points is well taken. Unless we find things in the world to be attractive or unattractive, it is hard to see why we would feel like doing anything. If any action we might perform, or its consequences, were wholly neutral in how it impressed us, why in the world would we do anything? Even the thought of suicide would be too neutral to motivate action. So, a grain of insight is found in the egoist's position. But is it strong enough to warrant the conviction that we do everything in order to gain pleasure or to avoid pain? No.

A fundamental difference arises between a necessary condition and the reason why we do something. Let us consider some necessary conditions for our doing what we do (whatever the particular action might be): we believe we can do it without suffering excruciating pain, we believe we can do it without going blind, we believe we can do it without our loved one being killed, and we believe it is possible for us to do it. Normally, we wouldn't do things unless we held the above beliefs. Who would go to work if they believed that doing so would kill their mother? Such facts or conditions serve to explain human behavior; they form the general background conditions of human existence and motivation. However true this may be, it still is incorrect to say that Chapman shot Lennon because he was alive, the world exists, he had air to breathe, he thought he could do it without suffering awful pain, or because he thought it was possible to shoot his victim. These are not the reasons or the motives for human action–even though we would not do anything unless such conditions existed.

The following is the best way to view the role of pleasure and pain in our lives. If nothing we did was in the slightest way pleasurable or painful to us–or promised to bring us some satisfaction–we would have no reason or incentive for doing anything. A similar point would be that unless attractive and unattractive things existed in the world, the world would be quite meaningless to us; it would make no difference what we did. Fortunately, the world is not put together in this neutered way; we are attracted or repelled. If we find it attractive to do something, if it pleases us to do so–this does not mean we do it in order to attain pleasure or avoid pain. Similarly, if we find it unattractive to do something, if it pleases us not to do it–this does not mean we avoid doing so in order to avoid pain or receive pleasure. For many reasons, an action may be attractive to us, including its production of pleasure for us, and its elimination of pain for us. But other reasons exist why it may be attractive: its production of pleasure for others, its elimination of pain for others, its being the right thing to do.

The best explanation of why I, for example, help a friend move out of a house may be that I want to help and I feel friends have such obligations to one another. Furthermore, (1) my helping out (or the thought of it) may bring me pleasure, (2) I would not have offered this help if it in no way pleased me to help out here, and yet my action may be unselfish. The fact that it pleases us to do something in no way implies that our action is selfish in moral terms. It may please us to do things which we know are painful or dangerous and bring little pleasure. It may please us to do such things because we think we have no choice, or because we think it is the right thing to do.

The egoist maintains that the best explanations of our behavior are in terms of pursuit of pleasure and avoidance of pain. The egoist is incorrect–if he or she argues that we do everything, at bottom, for these two reasons. Let's go through some cases. I would say the best explanation of a husband killing his wife's lover is his anger and jealousy, but I have no objection to adding that he did this because it pleased him to kill the fellow. But putting it this way is less revealing and less explanatory of the husband's action! It would be more natural and clarifying to say that it pleased him to do this because of his jealousy and anger.

Suppose a woman marries because she loves the fellow and wants to spend her life with him. The egoist will say she really does this because it pleases her. He gives her great pleasure and it would cause her great pain to lose him. I have no quarrel with saying she does this because it pleases her, but I would insist it pleases her to marry him because she loves him and wants to spend her life with him. Putting it this way is more natural and more informative than saying she did it because it pleased her.

Suppose I go to the grocery store, and the egoist says I do so because it pleases me. No doubt there is truth in this explanation, but is it more clarifying than saying that I do so in order to get my shopping done? Wouldn't it even be better to say that it pleases me to go to the store because I need to do some shopping?

Suppose a man rolls a joint because it pleases him to do so. He expects to get stoned. This is a good example of a case where it is quite true that a person acts in order to attain pleasure. It pleases him to roll the joint because he wants the pleasure of a high. So, it turns out, and it is no surprise to us, that people often do things simply (or mainly because) it pleases them to do so.

Why is the egoist's explanation in these cases supposed to be better than the ones I give? Do we gain more information about a person's motive for action if we know that it was done out of jealousy rather than because it pleased the person to so-act? Do we gain more information about a person's action if we know it was done out of love rather than because it pleased the person? Do we know more about my motivation if we know I went to the store in order to get groceries than if we know it pleased me to go to the store? Even in the hedonist's case, we learn more about his motive if we know he wanted to get stoned than if we know it pleased him to roll the joint. We gain more information by using my (modified common sense) model for explaining our actions. How is the egoist theory a deeper kind of explanation?

People are inclined toward things they find attractive and disinclined toward things they find unattractive. This is "the deep psychological truth" here. But since attractive things include not only sensations of pleasure (say, sexual pleasure), but beauty, order, liberty, kindness, honesty, we can hardly say that we act only in order to attain pleasure. Since unattractive things include not only sensations of pain (say, from a toothache), but ugliness, chaos, slavery, cruelty, and dishonesty, we can hardly say that we act only to avoid pain or receive pleasure.

Even if we occasionally do things we do not enjoy, and even if we sometimes do what we would prefer not to do "for others," the egoist will maintain that we choose to do what we most prefer to do given the circumstances we are in. A similar view of human psychology has been endorsed by thinkers as different in their perspectives as Plato and Sartre.[11] The egoist's idea here is that since we always choose to do what we most prefer (given the menu of options before us), we are indeed always self-centered, hence selfish, in our actions. I have already argued against inferring selfishness from self-concern,[12] but I want to examine this view nevertheless. This view amounts more to a metaphysical bias than to anything for which we can have good evidence.

Suppose a woman is tortured by security police in order to gain information on the location of her son, whom they suspect of being a rebel leader. After enduring a great deal, including rape and electric shock to her genital area, she tells them where she thinks he is. Has she done what she most wants to do given her terrible circumstances? Many of us will say, no. She most wants to protect her son. The egoist will disagree, arguing instead that though she greatly wants to protect her son, she wants even more to be free of continued torture. Hence, though understandable and not blameworthy, she acts selfishly–just as we all do whenever we act.

What evidence does the egoist have to prove this dubious contention? The egoist and I agree on all of the other facts here, yet we draw different conclusions about whether the woman did what she most wanted to do. I can imagine only two sorts of evidence to which we could appeal to decide this case. One, we could appeal to reflection on our experience of making difficult choices. Think about this case, compare it with your own choice-making experiences, then judge which is more plausible. Did she do what she most wanted to do–given her choices–or not? Two, consider the more general principle: when there are several competing influences, the most powerful of these will prevail. If we reflect on this generalization, our reason and our intuition judge it to be eminently plausible. Now apply this generalization to the case at hand. The woman is torn by contrary desires. Her desire to withhold the information and protect her son cannot serve to explain her *giving* the information to her torturers (and let us suppose she told them the truth). Some other, more powerful desire must have brought about her choice. In this situation, her desire to escape further agony is the most plausible candidate.

Neither of these arguments prove the egoist's point. Concerning the first, when I consult my experience, I am quite doubtful that I always do what I most prefer to do. I would always prefer to do what is best for me, and I would always prefer to act honorably and courageously. Unfortunately, I sometimes choose to do *what I consider to be* (at the time I make the choice) the less wise, less honorable, or less courageous of my alternatives. My reflection tells me I do this because I become infatuated with the pleasure of one of my (less desirable) options, because I am oppressed by the pain of one of my (less desirable) options, or because I am fearful of one of my (less desirable) options. In short, pleasure, pain, or fear can cause me not to choose what I would most prefer to choose. I imagine that many others will arrive at the same judgment. Egoists will be unable to prove their point by using this avenue of appeal.

The second argument rests upon the presumption that the most powerful psychological cause of a choice (at least, where the cause is intentional) equals what we most prefer to do. This is not a self-evident truth. We are complicated creatures with complex motivational structures, and I don't know why we should think our will should always succeed in producing actions in conformity with our will. I see even less reason for thinking our will to do what we think is most desirable should always succeed in this way. We have evidence that we all-too-often end up doing (accidentally or unknowingly) things which contradict our will. We want to cheer someone up with a joke, yet it only saddens or offends. We try to please a lover with flowers only to cause suspicion that we have ulterior motives for the gift. We try to be more efficient by doing something faster only to spill coffee on a customer, break a piece of china, injure ourselves so that we are unable to perform the task, etc. In our previous example, we may easily suppose the tortured woman most wants to withhold the information, but finds she is unable to because the pain is too powerful (hence she does what she least prefers to do). Thus, she does what she "wants" (intends) to do in the coercive circumstances, but not what she most wants to do.

I am willing to admit that the egoist's interpretation might be correct, but we have equally good reason for rejecting it in favor of mine. The egoist's interpretation is not obviously supported by the facts. Neither the observable data, experiential facts nor reason uniquely determines the truth of the egoist's view. What we face here are two metaphysical, competing theories of human motivation. I am content to point out that we have good reasons for doubting the egoist's theory.

5. Conclusion

It is not enlightened to believe that we ought to act selfishly because we cannot act otherwise. We *can* act considerately of others. The egoist confounds self-concern with selfishness and self-disregard with unselfishness. Unselfish action is showing a balanced concern for yourself and others. We should continue to praise and encourage unselfishness (when properly understood). The more we all act selfishly, the more we will all be treated inconsiderately. This is not desirable for others or yourself.

Egoism does have one positive insight. It is good to show concern for oneself. If people suggest to us that being considerate of our interests is selfish, we should not heed them. If they try to make us feel guilty for sometimes putting ourselves first, we should ignore them. Likewise, if others try to convince us that the only way to be "unselfish" is to neglect ourselves *for others*, we should remind them that we are just as important as others (morally speaking) and that being unselfish does not require us to be subservient to another's interest. For too long, one tradition within Christianity has insisted that the only path to virtuous living is the path of utter self-sacrifice and devotion to others. Such thinking is diseased and has poisoned too many of us. It is possible to conceive of egoism as an overreaction to this view, and to that extent egoism can be viewed as downright unhealthy. Our individual worth should not be swallowed up or annihilated by the herd. We should not only feel guilty for being inconsiderate of others, but also for being inconsiderate of ourselves.

We have lived through 1984, but Orwell's *1984*[13] is a dark reminder of the evils of "newspeak." Abbreviating speech, simplifying complex meaning, and reversing good and bad connotations can easily lead to more evil than intellectual confusion. The patriotic slogans of Orwell's *1984* were:

> Ignorance is strength.
> Freedom is slavery.
> War is peace.

It will not be a stroke of enlightenment if we make a nasty expression out of "unselfish" or a "double-plus-good" expression out of "selfish." Should society succumb to the philosophy of selfishness, our world will become even more unbalanced and ruthless.

Or in the spirit of Orwell, we may say: If you think only sticks and stones can break you, wait until you see what words can do to you.

Four

CHOICE AND RESPONSIBILITY

We could hardly take morality seriously if we did not also believe in human freedom and responsibility. Concepts like choice, coercion, compulsion, praise, blame, reward, and punishment are vital to the cultural heritage of Islam, Judaism, and Christianity. Like it or not, these traditions and the ancient Greek-Roman world-view continue to constitute the background for our ways of thinking about moral right and wrong.[1] The three major religions of the Western World emphasize the notion that each of us has free will and that as a result of this, we can be held accountable for our actions by God, other people, and ourselves. As a result, though most of us take it for granted that we are not free to do anything we please, we also believe our environment and genetic inheritance do not completely determine what we do. Being taught that we are created in the divine image, we assume this likeness implies we are basically free agents. No matter how restricted our range of choices may be (think of the imprisoned person or the slave), we believe that at any given time we have more than one option.

Is this true? Do we really possess "free will," or is this just a powerful myth entrenched by centuries of religious conditioning? Philosophers have debated this issue for a thousand years. Augustine (354-430 A.D.) argued we are free and responsible agents even though everything we are (and do) is determined ultimately by God's will.[2] He argued "acting freely" means we act in accord with our will, and we certainly are usually able to do what we mean to do. They have not achieved consensus about the correct answer or about how we should go about deciding the correct answer. They have made some progress in clarifying the issues involved and the possible solutions.

1. The Traditional Debate

To understand the problem better, let us begin with an example. Suppose Samantha is a sales clerk who is confronted by a masked man pointing a pistol at her and demanding that she turn over all the store's cash or he will kill her. Suppose Samantha is frightened at the prospect and complies with his demand. Question: Does Samantha freely give him the money and is she morally accountable for her action? Some people would say yes, although they would grant she is under great pressure and would prefer not to give him the money. They would argue that she still had a choice; she could have chosen not to give him the money (even though she might well have been killed for her contrariness). They would argue that her environment (present and past) and heredity do not determine that the only thing she can do in these circumstances is give him the money. Even though she is quite frightened, her fear does not preclude her choosing not to give him the money. People can greatly fear the consequences of doing something, yet still do it. Her desires and attitudes may have significant influence on her without necessitating that she act in any particular fashion. We know that people resist their desires and longtime habits in order to change their ways. Each of us has "free will," which means that (contrary to other events and processes in nature) we can make choices that fly in the face of past conditioning, biological makeup, and current external pressures. As a consequence, we are morally responsible for most of our behavior, excluding biological reflexes and other processes over which we have no control. Let us call this view "libertarianism."

Others maintain that Samantha does not act freely or in a way for which can she be held morally blameworthy. Oddly enough, they do not maintain this *because* of the coercion she suffers from the threat on her life. Instead, they ask us to focus on *causes* of her action: the thief's menacing behavior, her fear, and her desire to survive this incident. They ask us to recall that whatever happens in the world has a cause. Thus, causes exist of the thief's behavior and frame of mind, as well as causes of Samantha's possessing the temperament she possessed. All events are caused, and all causes are themselves the effects of other causes. In the case of human beings, this means that all of our present behavior is the causal result of a complex series of internal causes (physiological or psychological) and external causes. In the final analysis, this also means that what produces our actions is external to us, since even our hereditary characteristics are passed on to us by our parents.

Consider a crude analogy. Although human beings are not much like billiard balls (we are vastly more complicated), still the causes of billiard balls' behavior can be likened to the causes of our behavior. The cue ball strikes the five ball and causes the five ball to strike the nine ball, sending the nine ball into a corner pocket. What causes the nine ball to fall into the corner pocket?

True, the five ball's movement is a cause, but no such movement would have occurred unless the cue ball struck the five ball. In the last analysis, the movement of the cue ball is what made the nine ball drop into the corner pocket. Did the nine ball have any alternative? Did the five ball? No, they were made to behave as they did by their causes–factors external to them.

The cause of an event is what makes that event happen. The cause is what necessitates its effect. Let us put two and two together here. If all of our actions and states of mind are caused (made to happen), by factors which are, in the last analysis, external to us and beyond our control–how can we be free or morally accountable agents? Our desires, hopes, expectations, intentions–our very consciousness–are merely the effects of an enormous chain of causes. Our deeds and intentions are the products of the universe. The tail does not wag the dog. Therefore, human free action, free will, and personal responsibility are only illusions. Powerful illusions to be sure, but illusions nevertheless. Let us call this view "hard determinism."

Is there a third alternative, for judging our freedom and accountability? Yes, but before considering this perspective, let us dwell on the first two. This issue is not about legal, political, or cultural freedom. Our society's customs and laws prohibit and permit us various actions. In the United States, for example, we are free to drive the make of car of our choice (Toyota, Ford, Dodge, etc.), to express our opinions, and to wear the clothing of our choice–all subject to some limitations. We are not free to kill people we don't like, to drive 100 m.p.h. on highways or to sing the national anthem with ridicule as the guest performer at a major league baseball game. To say we were free to do the above is to say we can expect no legal or cultural penalties if we do them. To say we are not free to do the above is to say legal or cultural taboos are associated with doing them. We can expect some form of censure or punishment from violating these taboos. In my earlier example, the thief violates societal taboos by his action while the salesclerk does not. The issue is: does he freely commit his transgression, and does the salesclerk freely acquiesce to his demands? Furthermore, are they personally responsible for the choices "they" make?

How are we to decide this question? It seems that either the libertarian or the hard determinist must be right, while one of them must be wrong. We feel as though we have a great deal of control over what we do. It does not seem that anyone or anything else is manipulating our thoughts and behavior. We feel free and responsible for much of what we do. It is hard to consider seriously giving up our belief in our free agency. Imagine the consequences! No longer would we feel personally responsible for anything good or bad done by us. We might still have such feelings, but we would quickly reject their reliability–much like an illusion in the sun or a bad dream. No one would be held morally accountable for their actions–except perhaps on consequentialist grounds that doing so helped protect or improve society. Punishment and reward would not be thought to reflect individual merit, but merely a way of discouraging some kinds of behavior while encouraging others.

The transition from our traditional attitudes to this "brave new world" would be quite unsettling for many of us. We don't mind so much giving up personal responsibility for the bad things we have done, but we would like to take some responsibility for the good we have done. If reason should persuade our hearts that we are neither free nor responsible agents, this undoubtedly would be a blow to the self-esteem of many of us. This battering down of our self-image is the final step of our humiliation. Children are forced to see they are not the center of the world. Humanity was forced to concede that the Earth is not the center of the universe. The concept of God (hence our importance as God's creatures) is deadened by science and technology. Now comes the last straw: we are not even our own center. Instead, we are told our actions are only the periphery of the vast, centrifugal forces of the universe (present and past). Such counsel is bound to be the source of great despair for many. How far we have fallen!

Nevertheless, a feeling that we are free agents is not much to go on. What evidence do we have to back up this cherished belief? The hard determinist has a plausible case. We do believe that everything in nature has a cause, and we do think of causes as what explains their effects. This being so, how can we comfortably avoid the conclusion that everything we do, think, or feel is the product (ultimately) of factors beyond our control? It would appear our only resort is to imagine we are somehow not a part of nature, that our "free wills" are supernatural endowments from God. Still, this is to fortify a feeling by appeal to another feeling–to support a questionable conviction by an even grander article of faith. This may be okay for our hearts, but our sense of reason will find this maneuver highly suspect. In any event, in our contemporary world, how many of us can any longer believe in God? We may be sentimental about God, even respectful, but this does not mean faith in God is still alive for us. We bring flowers to the cemetery without believing that our loved ones are still alive.

Here is the problem in a nutshell. In spite of the longings of our hearts, are we reasonable to believe we are free and responsible agents? The hard determinist reminds us of our common sense faith in causality, then asks us to draw the implied conclusion for our "free will." Reflecting on this creates a dilemma for both our reason and our emotions. If we accept the hard determinist position, and it appears quite reasonable, then our cherished belief in our freedom and responsibility seems no more substantial than a ghost story, a centuries-old superstition. And most of us do want to see ourselves as reasonable. But, we are also reasonable to resist radical changes in the way we view ourselves and the world. Such changes can be disorienting and weaken our ability to adapt and survive. Rejecting our belief in our freedom and responsibility would be a radical change. Can we really be confident such a change in our world-view is warranted by the abstract reasoning of hard determinism? Maybe a subtle, yet vital, flaw exists in their argument. Maybe we ought not to be hasty, especially when the hard determinist conclusion can be so damaging to our self-esteem. Yet, habits–bad or good–are hard to change, and perhaps we are just being stubborn. Maybe the hard determinist argument is just what it seems–based on common sense and solid as a rock. What are we to believe?

Aside from the perspectives of libertarianism and hard determinism, we must consider another way of viewing this issue. According to this third position, libertarians and hard determinists have conflated two related concepts: causation and compulsion. As a result, they have mistakenly thought that the nature of free action (acting of our own "free will") and moral responsibility were incompatible with our being causally determined. (Hard determinists and libertarians can be called "incompatibilists'" for this reason.) But, according to this third perspective, an action of ours can be both freely done and caused. There is no incompatibility between our actions being caused and our freely doing them. If "being caused" amounted to "being coerced or compelled," matters would be different. As it stands, the truth is that while all compelled actions are caused, many caused actions are not compelled. Let us call this third alternative "compatibilism."

Recall my example of the salesclerk and the robber. Compatibilists would judge that Samantha did not act of her free will because her choice was coerced by the nature of the robber's threat to her life. Scenario One: She did not want to give him the money, and she did so only to avoid being shot. In other words, she really had no choice. Scenario Two: Had the would-be robber merely demanded the money without threatening her, and had she then given him the money, she would have acted freely.

Can she be blamed for her action? In the first Scenario, we would not be reasonable to hold her morally responsible, but in the second case, we would. What matters is not whether her behavior was caused, but the kind of causes involved. Some are coercive, others are not. When people do things because they enjoy doing so, their actions are caused by the anticipated pleasure, but they nevertheless do them of their free will. The debate between libertarians and hard determinists is just a confused, philosophical tangent–a metaphysical hubbub which confounds causal necessity with the kind of compulsion required to nullify our freedom and moral accountability.[3]

2. My View

Although I once believed in libertarianism (and on a few occasions, hard determinism seemed correct to me), I am now persuaded by a compatibilist point of view. Before we are exposed to the philosophical debate over our freedom (and usually afterwards), free versus un-free choice seems to involve the following considerations: (1) Did the persons know what they were doing? (And to what extent?) (2) Did they mean to act in that way? (Or was it an accident?) (3) Do they enjoy doing that sort of thing? (Or do they greatly dislike that sort of thing?) (4) Did another person get them to behave in that way by terrorizing them? (5) Did they realize they could have acted otherwise without serious harm coming to someone or something they cared for? (6) Were they hypnotized or unwittingly manipulated by other people to act in that way? Noticeably absent from our real-life judgments about human free action is a concern about whether people's choices are caused. Whether the concern is a legal one or an everyday judgment, we just don't think it important that a person's free action has causes. This is largely because we assume there are causes of all of our actions, whether free or un-free. I am sure that we would want to make the distinctions implied in (1)-(6) even if we were convinced that all of our behavior was "causally necessitated." These facts make me suspect that our concept of human free action is based on criteria (and contrasts) that do not depend on our action being free from causation. This hunch is typical for compatibilists.

Something similar can be said concerning our concept of personal responsibility for our attitudes and actions. However, our understanding of "free versus un-free" does not precisely parallel our understanding of "responsible versus not responsible," at least in cases where blame or punishment may be appropriate. We are prepared to judge people responsible for anything they do freely, but we are also prepared (in good conscience) to find people blameworthy in cases where they do not act freely. Ignorance of what we do implies we do not freely do it, but we also think that ignorance is not always an excuse. For example, if I accidentally run over a pedestrian while driving in a drunken stupor, I will be held morally responsible even though I did not mean to kill the person (and may not have known I had done so until much later when I sobered up). I did freely do other things which led to my homicidal behavior, but I did not kill the person (who could have been my best friend) of my free will. In order for us to do something of our free will, we must will it (not just cause it to be), and we cannot will it unless we intend it.

Aside from such cases of ignorant or accidental action, some cases arise where we are ready (in good conscience) to hold people blameworthy for acting under severe duress. Think of the severe honor code of the military. A soldier may be so frightened (perhaps even "paralyzed" by fear) that he or she fails to carry out a superior's order, or runs away from the battle. The soldier may quite plausibly argue that the action was involuntary (especially if he or she deeply believes in and desires to conform to military ethics), yet the soldier may be held morally blameworthy nonetheless. This severe code of responsibility was designed for the unusual demands of the life-and-death circumstances of war.

The relationship between our concept of free action and moral responsibility is the following. If we act freely, then we are personally responsible for our action. This is not to say we think we should be morally praised or blamed for all of our free actions, since many of the things we do day-in and day-out are beyond the sphere of moral concern. To act freely is to act intentionally and without being compelled, coerced, or manipulated. To say that people are free agents or have "free will" is to say that they are capable of acting freely and typically do act freely. But, if we do not act freely, this by itself does not tell us that we are not morally responsible for the action. It does indicate that due to ignorance, accident, coercion, compulsion, or manipulation, mitigating circumstances should reduce our degree of moral praise or blameworthiness.

Having said this much, the case for compatibilism is not yet proved. For one matter, we have not said enough about what makes people responsible for their actions. How would compatibilists analyze this issue? Both libertarians and the hard determinists have a clear-cut answer to when we are (or would be) personally accountable for our behavior. If we know what we are doing and we "have a choice," then we are responsible for what we do. To "have a choice" in performing an action at a particular time means that we could have done otherwise. Thus, if our salesclerk Samantha had a choice in her unfortunate circumstances, she could have done something other than giving the robber the money. This, in turn, means that her actions were not causally determined by factors external to her, that they did not necessitate her acting as she did. Since libertarians believe we do have such choice, such free will, they will say she was responsible for her action. Since the hard determinists believe we never have such choice, they will say she was not responsible for her action. Thus, the incompatibilist perspective on moral responsibility offers us a straightforward way of deciding when (if ever) people have a choice in what they do. Do compatibilists have an alternative account which is more credible?

The truth is that compatibilism does not have a simple and precise account of human free action and moral responsibility. I believe this is not a fatal flaw of compatibilism, but a reflection of the vagueness and complexity inherent in our ordinary understanding of freedom and responsibility. Both freedom and responsibility come in degrees, and like colors, the world of human behavior is not a "black and white" world. Contrary to mathematical concepts of triangularity, circularity, rectangularity, etc., we don't have a single, unified concept of what makes an action free or people responsible for their behavior.

Consider first the "shades" of freedom and responsibility. Do the people know what they are doing? We cannot expect that people know everything they do when they act. Suppose I intervene in a violent argument between a married couple who are my friends. I physically put myself between them and even try to restrain the woman from striking the man. What do I "do" here, and what do I know I am doing? I intervene and try to restrain my female friend, but I also do other things as a result of doing these two things. For example, I may make her furious at me, make him furious at me, and ruin my own evening. May we suppose I know I will do *those* things by jumping between my two friends? Perhaps I do, perhaps I do not. Consider what else I may do by jumping into this fracas. Unbeknownst to me, my male friend may have clutched a knife, and as I jump in between them to restrain her, he may lunge at her with the knife stabbing me in the back and puncturing my heart. Did I knowingly jeopardize my very life? Perhaps, but probably it was something I did not consider and would not have thought likely. The point is that whenever we act, we bring about many things of which we are unaware and had no reason to believe would occur. In order to act freely and to be morally responsible for our actions, we do not and should not expect that we have perfect knowledge of our actions and all of their ramifications.

Still, we must have some knowledge of what we are doing if we are to act freely and be held accountable for our action. In between having no knowledge of what we do and having perfect knowledge is a continuum of possible cases in which we are partly knowledgeable and partly ignorant of what we do. This fact about us means we are bound often to be quite unsure whether to judge that so-and-so knowingly did what he or she did. This hesitance or ambivalence is due to the fact that we are treating "acted knowingly" as an absolute all-or-nothing property when it is, in fact, a relative and mixed property.

A similar point can be made about whether we mean to act as we do, whether we are coerced by others, or whether we are in some way compelled to so act. Suppose my dear friend is about to step into the line of an on-coming car. Seeing this, I violently push him in the other direction, and as a result he breaks his arm in the fall. Did I mean to break his arm? I would protest that I did not, but that I pushed him only to save him from being hit by the car. Often what we mean by saying "I meant to do it" is "I wanted to do it," or "I found it enjoyable to do so." It is also true that though I did *not want* to treat him violently, much less risk breaking his arm, I did want to protect him from the car, and to insure this I intentionally knocked him down. Therefore, we can say truly that: (1) I did not mean to injure him, (2) I did mean to spare him injury, and (3) I did mean to do what I believed would spare him the greatest injury. The distinction between our overall goal in acting and the means we intend to bring these goals about is sufficient to generate degrees of meaning-to-do-something.

Coercion and compulsion also come in degrees. How much coercion or pressure is applied to people to get them to act as they do? Were they bribed with offers of petty cash, beaten, tortured, or threatened with such treatment? If they were merely threatened with such treatment, how likely did they think it was that the threat would be carried out? Were they paralyzed with fear, immobilized by severe pain, suffering significant fear or pain, suffering mild pain or fear, or only somewhat concerned about their circumstances? If addiction led to their behavior, was it physical or psychological addiction? How strongly addicted were they? Cold-turkey withdrawal from alcohol is more severe than cold-turkey withdrawal from heroin or tobacco. If they were manipulated by others, how direct was it? How persuasive and persistent? If we treat the concept of coercion or compulsion as an absolute, all-or-nothing affair, we will seek unequivocal judgments about whether a person was or was not coerced, when the reality is often that the person was coerced in some ways but not in others. In cases where people are under coercion or compulsion, our question should not be whether they acted of their own free will, but *to what extent* were they compelled to act as they did. Having decided this issue, we can then decide whether it is fair, humane, or reasonable to hold them personally responsible for their actions.

The degree to which people act freely is not the only issue which clouds our ability to decide whether they act freely. Centuries of religious teachings and our naive tendencies in constructing our view of the world lead us to think that a singular and objective reality exists which constitutes our ability to act freely. This is our free will, which makes us god-like and distinguishes us from other creatures. We imagine that our free will can be influenced and tempted, but not compelled, by anything external to it. This may be true, but unfortunately this paradigm of free action is not the only one which appeals to us. We also think it is important that people know what they are doing if they act freely, that they mean to do it, and more. What kind of a "choice" a person confronts is also vital to us. Our salesclerk from the earlier example can "choose" to resist the thief if she is willing to risk being murdered. Since our general will is to be able to do otherwise without losing our lives, we think of this as being no choice at all. We might well say of such a case, "She had no choice but to give him the money." When others force our choices in this way, we think of the circumstance as one where we do not act of our own will, but due to the will of the coercer. Here then is another paradigm of "acting of our own free will." To do so is to be free from such coercion by others.

The problem is that other paradigms of free action exist which imply different criteria for acting freely. What if our environment compels us (if we are to survive) to act in a way we detest? If I believe stealing is morally evil, but do so only to feed myself or my children (because I am unemployed and welfare services are non-existent for me), many of us will judge that I do not freely choose to be a thief. Here, my "choices" again leave me between a rock and a hard place, but coercion by others is not involved. Another paradigm of free action emerges–being free from environmental coercion.

Still other paradigms are significant to us: not being compelled by mental illness, not being hypnotized to act as we do, and not being manipulated by others in certain ways. We could try to overcome this difficulty by stipulating that people must be free from all of these constraints if they are to act freely. This will not work because many people are convinced that all of these complications cloud an overriding fact: what counts most is whether a person can choose to do otherwise, no matter how severe the penalty. And this ability, they will say, means we almost always do act freely because we almost always have more than one option we can select.

So who is right? Which of these views of free action is correct? I think there is no way to reasonably decide this, and we are misguided to believe one of these views must be "the correct view."[4] Each view focuses on ways in which our behavior or state of mind can be constrained, ways in which our choice is restricted, and each of these kinds of constraints are significant to us. For example, when we are concerned to assess moral praise or blame, the presence of environmental coercion or coercion by others is relevant as an indication of mitigating circumstances. Thus, we should be prepared to lessen our assignment of praise or blame for the action under scrutiny. A person who gives money to charity because of blackmail is not noble or admirable for such "generosity." A person who gives the money belonging to others to a thief is not blameworthy if this was done to avoid being murdered. It can also be useful to recall that we almost always have the ability to choose otherwise–even if subject to terrible coercion. No law of nature or logic exists which makes it true that people have to give in to coercion, even severe coercion. A person can chose to accept the pain or loss of life. We are "only human," but being human does not determine that we must succumb. No matter how unlikely and no matter what our past choices have been, each of us has the capability to be heroic. Realizing (or believing) this about ourselves can boost our self-esteem and give us motivation to be stronger in the future.

Instead of debating whether we truly act of our free will, we would do better to consider what our behavior is free from. If we meant to insult our father and would have done otherwise had we chosen to, then our action was free from ignorance and under conscious control. In this sense of "acting freely," we acted freely. If we were not coerced by others to do this, we acted freely in another sense of the expression. If our decision to insult our dad was free from hypnotic suggestion or other devious thought-control by others, then we acted freely in another sense of "free choice."

Are we ever free from all limitations or constraints on our behavior? No. There is no complete or perfect freedom. Our options are confined by environmental limitations as well as our own physical and psychological limitations. I am not free to jump vertically twenty feet in the air, nor to run a one minute mile. We are born, live, and die within many constraints. The essential point, for practical and moral purposes of assessing personal responsibility, is to be clear on the kinds of limitations which lead us to think and behave as we do.

The pluralistic nature of our concept of free action does not mean it is hopeless to decide when people should be held morally accountable for their behavior. Knowing what kinds of factors influenced people to behave as they did can help us decide the extent (if any) to which we shall hold them morally responsible. Whether our conception of free choice emphasizes people's knowledge of what they do, the rationality of their choices, the lack of external coercion or manipulation–each centers on the importance of being in control of their choice. Thus, we can say that the more control we exert over our choices, the more responsible we are. The less control we have, the less responsible we are. To decide whether to censure or punish others for their choices, we can apply the Golden Rule (or the Hypocrisy-Avoidance) test. Would we have behaved any differently if we were tortured? Would we have allowed ourselves to get into the drunken state that precipitated this fellow's accidentally running over a child? If we can sincerely answer that we would have behaved differently, we will be justified in blaming a person for failing to resist torture or for having drunkenly killed a child. We also need to ask ourselves if we would blame ourselves if we behaved in such a way. If we would (and it can be difficult to be honest with ourselves about this), then it is fair for us to blame someone else for such behavior. Such considerations will also give us guidance in deciding how harsh or forgiving our response to wrongdoing should be. Such a procedure will allow for a realistic inclusion of both justice and mercy in our assessment of moral responsibility. Even if I am better able to resist torture than another, and even if I would not allow myself to become so recklessly drunk, I must still recognize the (mitigating) extent to which the other did not act freely. While this model of assessing responsibility and blame moves us away from the black-and-white view that for any of our choices, we are totally responsible for them or we are not responsible at all, it does allow us to retain a substantive correlation between choice and moral responsibility.

A second issue has made the compatibilist perspective even more dubious to many. Hard determinists and libertarians can quite credibly insist that the most I have shown so far is that our ordinary concept of human freedom and responsibility is different from what we should expect it to be if we conscientiously pursued the implications of our belief in causation. We believe that all natural events are caused, that causes explain their effects, yet we do not pay heed to what this implies for our lack of freedom and responsibility (if all of our behavior is causally determined). We fail to be consistent, and we fail to put two and two together. Human beings often are inconsistent in their behavior and attitudes, but this hardly shows that the complete determination of our behavior is consistent with our being free and responsible agents.

I think compatibilists should reply as follows. It is true that people believe all events are caused. We are closed-minded to the hypothesis that some occurrences "just happen out of the blue." Ours is a cause-effect world. We think of the cause of an event as explaining why the event occurred and as that which was responsible for the event. Does all of this imply that we think of causes as making their effects necessary? Philosophers have long taken for granted that some kind of necessity links causes with their effects. In our century philosophers tend to think of the analysis of causation done by Hume and Kant,[5] but discussion of the necessity involved in causality goes back at least as far as Leibniz[6] in the seventeenth century and Aristotle in the fourth century B.C. This necessity raises problems for human freedom and responsibility.

So where is this necessity linking cause-effect relationships? Hume examined his experience and was unable to locate it.[7] Aside from a subjective expectation that what he called "cause" would be followed by what he called "effect," Hume could not pin down the necessity he linked to cause-effect relationships. He concluded that something in our idea of cause-effect relationships was foreign or extraneous to our experience of such relationships. For Hume, our idea of causation was far clearer than the notion that causes make their effects necessary.

Let us confirm this for ourselves. A boxer strikes another boxer in the face, knocking the second to the canvas. We think of the first boxer's punch as being the cause of the other's knock-down. Did we *observe* anything that informs us the first boxer's punch made it *necessary* that the second fall to the canvas? Do similar punches always have this effect (as we have observed them in the past)? Can we imagine that such a punch is thrown and connects, yet the person punched does not get knocked down? The answers are: "No, such punches have not always had this effect," and "Yes, we can imagine that the cause occurs, yet the effect does not." If we reflect on the wide variety of things we are prepared to call "cause-effect" relationships, we will realize that in many cases we would get the same answers to these two questions. Such reasoning led many philosophers in this century to abandon the notion that the necessity of cause-effect relationships was to be found in the world of our experience. Instead, they presumed that the necessity implied by cause-effect relationships was to be found in logical relationships presupposed by scientific explanations of causes and their effects. The philosopher of science, Carl G. Hempel[8] argued that every adequate scientific explanation of causal relationships presupposed the following three features: (1) a covering law of nature, (2) a description of the initial conditions, (3) and a statement describing the effect which is logically deducible from (1) and (2).

Consider an example. Suppose a rock thrown at a window causes it to break. If so, there must be a law of nature (a law which we may not know) to the effect that when an event occurs like a rock striking a window pane, the object struck will shatter. Let us call what is described in my last sentence after the word "when" and *prior to the second comma*, " the initial conditions." Now, if and when scientists discover this law of nature, they will be in a position–upon observing the initial conditions–to predict (logically deduce) with certainty that the object struck will shatter. They will know a kind of conditional (not absolute) necessity exists here: necessarily, *if* the initial conditions occur, the effect will follow. The law of nature states whenever *A*, then *B*, and if it is also true that *A*, it is inconsistent to suppose that *B* will not occur. We are not saying the effect is absolutely necessary (or it would occur all the time), but only that given its cause, it has to occur.

We now must ask ourselves whether our concept of causation implies the kind of necessity philosophical determinists have said it does. Does our understanding of cause-effect depend upon our believing the cause "necessitates" the effect in any sense? I cannot see that it does. The idea of necessity determining worldly events is a myth–promoted by those whose heart demands that the world be absolutely reasonable, predictable, and under control. To help make this point, consider the following argument advanced by Peter Van Inwagen (a libertarian).

> Suppose someone throws a stone at a window and that the stone strikes the glass and the glass shatters in just the way we should expect glass to shatter when struck by a cast stone. Suppose further that God reveals to us that the glass did not *have* to shatter under these conditions, that there are possible worlds having exactly the same laws of nature as the actual world in every detail up to the instant at which the stone came into contact with glass, but in which the stone rebounded from the intact glass. It follows from what we imagine God to have told us that determinism is false. But does it also follow that the stone did not break the glass, or that the glass did not break *because* it was struck by the stone? ...Wouldn't it be more reasonable to say this: that, while the stone did cause the window to break, it was not *determined* that it should; that it i*n fact* caused the window to break, though, even if all conditions had been precisely the same, it might not have?[9]

Given the difficulties we have in pinning down the supposed necessity which relates cause and effect, why must philosophers persist in holding on to a necessitarian paradigm of causal regularities? We could suppose that the essential connection between a cause and its effect is no stronger than *probability* (or perhaps high probability). We could suppose that the covering laws presupposed by causal explanations need only be prefaced by a probability operator. Such models of causation have been put forward by philosophers. Without eliminating the possibility that a cause makes its effect 100 percent certain, Rosen's account[10] would interpret the "force" of causation (the power of a cause to "make" its effect happen) as the cause raising the probability, given the relevant background conditions, that the effect will occur.

One contemporary advocate of strict determinism, Ted Honderich, argues that to abandon strict determinism is to abandon conceiving of events as causes and effects. He is not impressed by Van Inwagen's thought-experiment about the broken window. "It seems to me a small scandal that this sort of persuasion... should convince anyone to contemplate the idea that we have any such ordinary idea of causation."[11] Even if we dress up indeterminism in probabilistic attire, Honderich argues that it is absurd to speak of effects and causes without the supposition that effects are necessitated by their causes. Why is this absurd? He offers several reasons, including a specific set of arguments against probabilistic theories[12] of causation. Of these, his most basic and strongest objections are the following. Without supposing the cause necessitates its effect, we would have (1) no explanation of the so-called "effect" and (2) no basis for thinking that causes "make" their effects happen.

Before responding to (1) and (2), I want to say that I do not think van Inwagen's thought experiment is absurd. I find it persuasive. It shows that pre-philosophically we are far more convinced of the reality of some cause-effect relationships than we are of the precise implications of such relationships.

Concerning (1) why should we think that, absent the presumption of causal necessity, "there exists no explanation whatever"[13] of the event in question? Does Honderich suppose that, in general, a minimal requirement of any good explanation must be that it shows why only that *explandum* could be true? If so, his presumption is not plausible. Consider historical explanations and ordinary human action explanations. They don't usually meet such a stringent requirement. Instead of purporting to show why some state of affairs *S* had to be as it was, they usually purport to show why *S* was not surprising (why it made sense) given the antecedent conditions. Thus, we might read that Nixon decided to negotiate an end to the Vietnam War because public support for the war had dropped to a very low level. Likewise, we might hear that a person killed his wife's lover because the husband was insanely jealous. In both cases, the reason given helps us see the event as understandable given such prior conditions. You could point out that in both cases, there must have been "more to it than that," but such a truism would not nullify the credibility of the explanations.

In historical explanations and ordinary human action explanations, we could always point to many causal antecedents as bringing about, or helping to bring about, the event in question. We can go back further in time, or we can focus on the immediate, causal background conditions. Which conditions we pick out will depend on our interests and needs. Our criteria for the adequacy of such explanations usually include truth and relevance of the explanation offered. A crucial part of the relevance-test is that the explanation cite conditions which were necessary to the occurrence of the event in question.[14] Absent is the demand that the explanation show why that particular event had to happen. If this is so for these kinds of explanations, why do we have to suppose that causal explanations require a more rigid standard?

Why not consider causal explanations to be underwritten by probability rather than necessity? Because, says Honderich, this gives us no basis for thinking that causes "make" their effects happen–his objection (2). "It is not too much to say that the probabilistic analyses must revise this into a belief that many effects are *not made* to happen."[15]

Does a probabilistic view of causation undermine our ordinary conviction that causes "produce" their effects or "make" them happen? I think our ordinary causal convictions are fuzzier and more ambivalent about this than Honderich suggests. We do often speak as if the cause makes the effect occur, as if once the cause is in place, nothing can prevent the effect from happening. But on the probabilistic model, it seems we are warranted only in saying that the cause makes its effect likely, not that it makes it occur. Perhaps, then, we should admit that a price the probabilistic account requires us to pay is a substantial revision of our causal convictions. Whether we would be willing or able to pay this price is another matter. I suspect this would not present a great problem for most people, though it might be psychologically impossible for some intellectuals. Strict determinists would, no doubt, react to such a proposed revision as if it meant absurdity and nihilism. I think this would be an overreaction.

When we are not theorizing about our concept of causation, we often speak of *x* having caused *y* where we mean the following: *y* came from *x*, emerged from *x*, or *x* gave birth to *y*. Here the cause is conceived of as if it were a fertile garden or brew which made conditions ripe for the occurrence of the effect. Thus, poor insulation may be cited as the cause of a fire, an intense weather system as the cause of a tornado, or a driver's being tired as the cause of his car accident. Where we suppose a series of temporally ordered causes, we pick out *x* as being the immediate cause of *y* because (as Hume suggested) *x* is proximate to *y* in space and time and *y* did not exist prior to *x*.

In any event, there is another perspective to consider. We also often speak of causes as if they can "make" their effects happen even though they didn't have to make those effects happen. In other words, we think *x* was sufficient for the effect *y*, but we are non-committal about whether *x* is, or will always be, sufficient for *y*. Here common sense seems vindicated by logic. The proposition, "Ten dollars was sufficient to pay for filling my gas tank," hardly entails, "Ten dollars is now sufficient to pay for filling my gas tank." In general, what is now and what was sufficient are different classes of things. We are especially likely to think of causes being sufficient in this (limited) way in cases where the cause is dynamic and fairly complex. Such statements are made not only with regard to human beings, but also with regard to some other things. We typically think that people are the authors of many of their actions, and that they need not have behaved in those ways. People who study chimpanzees and dolphins attribute the same sort of causality to them as well. Pet lovers would likely say that much of their pets' behavior also should be so categorized. This point can be extended to non-living systems and the micro-level. Consider the causality of an egg being penetrated by a sperm. One sperm out of millions manages to penetrate the egg. Biologists believe the sperm causes the egg's breach, but they will not suppose that *that* sperm had to have that effect. Finally, we suppose stormy weather systems produce various events (floods, forest fires, and tornadoes), but we don't think the weather system had to have exactly those effects.

The strict determinist will seek to explain away such examples as the results of human ignorance, fuzzy-thinking, or inconsistency. Perhaps they are correct, but they may be attempting to force our pluralistic and imprecise concept of causality into a more uniform and precise mould. Let us recall Aristotle's analysis of "cause."[16] He maintained that the wise philosopher should pay heed to the ways in which people actually speak about the world. When he presented his analysis of the ordinary Greek way of conceptualizing causation, he said a cause is an answer to a "why-question." In other words, citing *x* as the cause of *y* was supposed to provide an explanation of *y*. But he cited four different kinds of causes: the efficient cause, the material cause, the formal cause, and the final cause. Of these, only the first approximates the modern determinist theory of a cause being *sufficient* for its effect, of "making" the effect happen. The most we could say of material and final causes is that they serve as necessary conditions of the effect. If I am correct, then we might deny Honderich's contention that a probabilist model of causation forces us to substantially revise our causal convictions. In particular, we might deny the need to abandon our conviction that causes "make" their effects happen. Instead, we could maintain that in causal relationships, if *x* makes *y* likely and *y* occurs, then *x* makes *y* occur. In other words, a cause not only makes its effect likely, it also often makes it occur (given the cause). To accept this way of thinking would mean that the power of a cause to produce its effect is not fully analyzable. To this extent, the power of causal "production" would remain ineffable. Still, we should recall what Hume said of our idea of necessary connection: "We have no idea of this connection, nor even any distinct notion what it is we desire to know when we endeavor a conception of it."[17]

Our modern concept of cause still reflects the plurality noticed by Aristotle (not that our concept is exactly like that of ancient Greek culture). For example, a typical answer to why people act as they do involves citing their goals or purposes. Typical answers to such why-questions involve citing what in those circumstances provoked so-and-so to act as he or she did. A person may be depressed for a long while, yet not attempt suicide. So we look for precipitating causes, (final rejection by a loved one) to explain the suicidal effort. On the other occasions, our interest turns to origins (our parents being the cause of our "being here"). On still other occasions, we focus on "essential" causes (the greedy side of human nature) to explain behavior. Many philosophers speak of "causes" (and causal explanations) in still other ways.

With reference to our conviction that all events are caused, our ordinary concept of cause concerns the relative origin of an event.

Thus, we think of the rock, or its movement, as the cause of the broken window, the wind as the cause of tree branches swaying, our parents as the cause of our existence, George Bush as a cause of American troops going to Saudi Arabia, etc. We think of effects as arising out of their causes. Thus, we are convinced that nothing comes from nothing: every event has a cause. We also associate a regularity with causes and their effects, but we do so without having concluded that this regularity must amount to invariability or necessity. Likewise, we imagine that causes "make" their effects happen, that they are the source "responsible for" their effects, and that they have "the power to produce" their effects, without having concluded that this means they necessitate their effects.

3. Pragmatic Compatibilism

What if, contrary to the conviction of compatibilists, determinism really does rule out that we ever act as free or morally responsible agents? What if everything in the world is so determined? What if the necessitarian model of causality is correct? I argue that for the *pragmatic* compatibilist, a question of prior importance is: How could we know whether any causal relationship is thusly determined? Peter Van Inwagen has expressed a similar doubt:

> I have a very hard time seeing why so many philosophers seem to think that the results of the empirical study of human beings lend support to the hypothesis that human behavior is determined. I do not mean that I believe that empirical investigations have shown that human behavior is not determined. My difficulty is simply this: the human organism and human behavior are such terribly complex things, and so little is known about the details of that terrible complexity (in comparison with what there is to be known), that it is hard to see why anyone should think that what we do know renders a belief that human behavior is determined reasonable. I can only conclude that these philosophers are convinced on *a priori* grounds, or perhaps on no real ground at all, that human behavior is determined, and, owing to this conviction, are predisposed to regard very nearly anything as evidence in support of it.[18]

Pragmatic compatibilism represents a significant departure from traditional compatibilism. Traditional compatibilists maintain that the following two propositions can both be true: (1) All worldly events or states of affairs are causally necessitated, (2) We are free and morally responsible agents. They believe that the kind of necessity involved in cause-effect relationships is irrelevant to the absence of compulsion required for us to act as free and responsible agents. I am not sure about this, and I know of no argument which demonstrates the irrelevancy of (1) to (2). Perhaps a necessary (but not sufficient) condition of our being free and morally responsible agents is that (1) is false (specifically at the level of human actions and mental states). If so, traditional compatibilism is mistaken. With this in mind, I propose a pragmatic amendment to compatibilism. The pragmatic compatibilist will maintain that what matters is not only "the truth," but what we are rationally justified in believing to be true. We can have good reasons for believing something even though (due to our human fallibility and limitations or to lacking enough evidence) our belief is false. We may, for example, have excellent evidence that a person is our friend, even though the person is not (but has tricked us into believing so for ulterior motives). We may have good reasons for believing there is no God or afterlife, but we may nonetheless be mistaken. Likewise, modern science rests on the acceptance of the revisability of theory and hypothesis, no matter how good the evidence currently is in favor of them, in the light of future evidence to the contrary.

Since we are not gods, the worthiness of our beliefs cannot be measured solely by the standard of whether they conform to the way the world really is. We need also pay heed to our happiness and our survival. Radical and rapid change, in belief or lifestyles, is extremely difficult for people, and it is quite reasonable to doubt whether we would be better off in every case to believe what is true if doing so threatened our psychological health or our very survival. In any event, I know of no argument which establishes that the value of truth should always outweigh every other value.

The kind of pragmatism I advocate does not forsake the value of striving to believe what is true, but only that we not be obsessive in our advocacy of truth, especially in cases where "the truth" at issue is far removed from our ability to know what is true and where what we believe is of vital concern to us. Human beings are biased toward some metaphysical issues which defy our ability to resolve with certainty. Among these, I would include the existence of God, an afterlife, and human free will. We can base our view of determinism on pragmatic criteria, taking our lead from William James:

> The pragmatic method is primarily a method of settling metaphysical disputes that otherwise might be interminable. Is the world one or many?–fated or free?–material or spiritual?– here are notions either of which may or may not hold good of the world; and disputes over such notions are unending. The pragmatic method in such cases is to try to interpret each notion by tracing its respective practical consequences. What difference would it practically make to anyone if this notion rather than that notion were true?[19]

I would also include the prevalent philosophical belief, which I share, that truth is valuable for "its own sake." If I am correct that such issues exist (and there are more than I have mentioned), how shall we rationally decide them? According to the pragmatic attitude I am suggesting, when the evidence fails us on these issues, our justification must be conservative with regard to protecting our psychological well-being. Thus, the "pragmatic" criteria I have in mind here are not the criteria understood by contemporary philosophers of science. Instead, I mean the consequences of a belief for human self-esteem and happiness. What boosts human self-esteem and happiness has positive pragmatic value. What erodes them has negative pragmatic value. Let us see how this approach applies to the issue of human freedom and moral responsibility.

How could we confirm the nature of the causality which exists in the universe? The alternative to the traditional determinist view of causality is that causality in the world does *not* involve invariable or necessary relationships between cause and effect. Indeterminism expresses a range of possibilities about causal regularities. At one extreme, it could be that the relationship is purely random, and at the other extreme, it could be that the correlation between cause and effect is highly probable. Some correlations between events could be lower than 1 out of 10, while others might be higher than 9 out of 10 (short of 100 percent).

How could we empirically decide between the determinist and indeterminist hypotheses? Our evidence would consist of what we could observe of cause-effect relationships. Suppose a virus is thought to cause a cancer in human beings. If traditional determinism is correct, we could expect that whenever this virus gains access to a human being (given background conditions or context) the human being develops that form of cancer. Thus, suppose we observed a sufficiently large sample of such exposures (say,

2000) and discovered that in each case the people exposed developed cancer. Based on our observations, a 100 percent correlation would exist between the occurrence of this cancer given the prior presence of the virus in people's bodies. Such evidence would confirm the view that we had discovered an exceptionless covering law. The problem is that such evidence would be equally supportive of a highly probabilistic connection between exposure to the virus and the cancer. For example, it might be that if we had observed 10,000 such cases, we would find that in 1000 cases the cancer did not develop, yielding a regularity of 90 percent. It might also be that the correlation was higher than 90 percent, but lower than 100 percent.

What if the regularity between cause and effect were .955555555? If so, the same observable evidence, for all practical purposes accessible to human observation, would be equally supportive of both the strict determinist correlation and the probabilistic alternative. In other words, the exception might occur so rarely that it is never observed by us. In any case, the number of repeatable scientific tests that are normally taken to be confirmation of a causal regularity (based on inductive generalization) fall far short of what it would take to distinguish between a probability of the magnitude of .955555555 versus a correlation of 100 percent. If we keep in mind the possibility of such probabilistic correlations, we see that generalizations (if we must construe them as exceptionless) made on the basis of available evidence are indeed leaps of faith.

But what about the case where an apparent exception to a Hempelian covering law is observed? Would not this refute the adequacy of such a law? I think not. The existence of such decisive observation-contexts is not a plausible option in the complex universe in which we live and within the metaphysically fluid framework of traditional determinism.

> It would appear easier. . .to refute a false hypothesis than to establish a true one. If a hypothesis implies observations at all, we may stand ready to drop the hypothesis as false as soon as an observation that it predicts fails to occur. In fact, however, the refutation of hypotheses is not that simple. . .It is not the contemplated hypothesis alone that does the implying, but rather that hypothesis and a supporting chorus of background beliefs...Discarding any particular hypothesis is just one of many ways of maintaining consistency in

> the face of contrary observation; there are in principle many alternative ways of setting out beliefs in order.[20]

The traditional determinist is always free to discount the alleged exception as due to presently undetected or unaccounted-for intervening variables. For example, suppose metal when heated has always been observed to expand in some background conditions, yet a case arises where *x* is observed to be metal and is heated, but *x* is observed not to expand. We are logically free to speculate that this is because the background conditions had changed, that we incorrectly observed *x* as a metal, or misperceived that *x* was heated, or that *x* really did expand contrary to our incorrect perception. Naturally, the more difficult it is for us to justify the presence of such intervening variables, the more people would conclude that such an explanation was invented just to save our pet theory. But if we were unable to explain plausibly the presence of such intervening variables, this still would not be decisive proof that our explanation was merely an invention to save our theory. The previous observations in support of "When metal is heated, it expands" might be so well-established, and the law might be so useful to the interlocking web of scientific theory and prediction that the scientific community would refuse to reject the law, dismissing instead that one observation-context as an isolated (and non-repeatable) anomaly produced by observational error. Indeed, if a scientist was to observe the rare case that would confirm a probability-uniformity on the magnitude of .955555555, the public repeatability requirement of science would guarantee the rejection of that one observation as somehow inaccurate! The case where the universal law is violated occurs so rarely that we could not expect to observe it again in countless trials set up to replicate the exceptional case. Thus, when other scientists set about to replicate those experimental conditions, they would not observe any violation of what seems to be an exceptionless law. The nature of the probability-uniformity would preclude confirmation by other scientists who sought to duplicate the result and who operated with the Hempelian model of causal laws.

Some readers may object that this strategy for defending the possibility of human free will depends upon a pathetic notion of freedom. How, they may wonder, can such a notion of our ability to do otherwise give any comfort if the truth is that in every case our chance of acting otherwise is as low as .044444445? My response is that nothing is pathetic about this conception of metaphysically possible choices. Especially for the purpose of defending our moral accountability for our actions, we need only maintain that–no matter how great the obstacles are to our choosing otherwise–our ability to do otherwise is not absolutely foreclosed. Circumstances can strongly incline us to behave in one way without necessitating that we do so. Resisting torture or a threat to our life is vastly more difficult than resisting peer pressure or personal insults. Nothing is pathetic in acknowledging that some circumstances make it extremely unlikely that a person will behave otherwise. Our ordinary way of conceiving "choice-contexts" have always included (as have defenders of free will) a recognition that degrees of predictability of human action are associated with degrees of pressure brought to bear on a person.

We should not conflate indeterminism with the view that all events, actions, or choices occur randomly. Indeterminism is merely the denial of the view that the world is regulated by necessity. Worldly events and human behavior may just as well, according to indeterminism, be regulated by degrees of probability. The libertarian defense of free choice does not require that genuine choices be made capriciously or at random. We normally believe that we can reliably predict a good deal of what people will freely choose to do. True, we might be disturbed if we thought all of our actions were determined as tightly as .955555555, but we have no reason to suppose that the probabilities are typically this great.

We should conclude that no practical way is available to confirm such a probabilistic connection over a necessary connection between a cause and an effect (or causal *explanans* and *explanandum*). Any evidence which might favor such a probabilistic correlation over a necessitarian view can reasonably be explained away by appealing to the great complexity of our world or our fallible human powers of perception. These are not new problems for epistemology or the philosophy of science. Even empiricists like Quine have devoted time and effort to explaining why we must abandon the verificationist dream of crucial experiments and decisive observation-contexts:

> The dogma of reductionism survives in the supposition that each statement, taken in isolation from its fellows, can admit of confirmation or infirmation at all...The totality of our so-called knowledge or beliefs from the most casual matters of geography and history to the profoundest laws of atomic physics or even pure mathematics and

> logic is a man-made fabric which impinges on experience only along the edges...The total field is so under determined by its boundary conditions, experience, that there is much latitude of choice as to what statements to reevaluate in the light of any single contrary experience.[21]

Suppose, then, that we cannot know whether traditional determinism ever is the proper interpretation of cause-effect relationships, where the effect is a human action or mental state. Would this uncertainty and ignorance undermine our common sense and scientific world-views? Hardly. Common sense and science both: (1) abhor chaos, and (2) desire the world to be uniform and predictable in (non-trivial ways) that we can discover through our experience. But both (1) and (2) are satisfied if causal regularities are merely probabilistic; neither depends on the truth of traditional determinism. Where correlations between a cause and its effect are less than 100 percent but greater than random–a circumstance which accords well with our common-sense experience of the world–we can still retain our confidence that the future will resemble the past. We don't doubt that speeding is a cause of many people's deaths just because not everyone dies who drives too fast. We will still expect that proper diets are a cause of good health and long life even though we know that some people remain sick and die at an earlier age who have received proper nourishment. We will still expect that a loss of "vital" bodily functions will result in a person's death even if, once every 2,000 years, a person returned to life after all vital signs had ceased for twenty-four hours. In this same vein, all that science requires for meaningful investigation and theory-construction is that humanly discoverable regularities exist in nature. The regularities need not be necessitarian. The laws of thermodynamics would still be scientific laws if they asserted probabilities rather than exceptionless certitudes. I conclude that no necessary connection exists (either common-sensically or scientifically) between our concept of causality and the thesis that causes necessitate their effects. Our concept of causation is not in any way jeopardized if traditional determinism is rejected as idle speculation or wishful thinking.

While science and common sense are not threatened by the loss of the traditional determinist's view of causality, common sense is threatened by the loss of our view that we usually act freely and are morally responsible for what we do. It is important to most people's self-esteem that they feel they have some control over their destiny and that their actions are not merely the results of external forces. We don't want to feel as though we are puppets of our heredity and environment. We are so convinced that we possess significant free will that we tend to dismiss philosophers' arguments to the contrary as verbal hocus pocus. But if we seriously thought that we had no free will, most of us would experience great anxiety, sadness, or depression. In a related way, to hold people morally accountable for their behavior is also important to us. Parents want to continue to have a good conscience about their punishment and reward of their kids' behavior (which is not to suggest they condone child abuse) in order to teach them how to become responsible adults. We want to have a good conscience about holding other adults (friends, lovers, strangers) morally responsible for their conduct. We also want to think it makes sense for us to hold ourselves responsible for what we do, that it is sensible sometimes to regret what we have done. Our legal institutions, customs, and our very way of life rest heavily on the presumption that the categories of freedom and responsibility apply to human beings. It is no exaggeration to say that we are determined to hold one another personally responsible for much of what we do. If it is difficult to imagine a planet free from war or violence, how much harder must it be to imagine a planet where most of us–including most intellectuals–cease to hold one another to be morally responsible agents!

4. Conclusion

A good portion of our sense-making scheme is wed to our common-sense commitment that we have free will, and our ways of feeling and behaving would be significantly affected if we came to believe that we have no free will. If we accept incompatibilism and we also accept traditional determinism, our common-sense world view is threatened.

These considerations give us solid pragmatic grounds for believing that we are free agents who can be held personally responsible for many of our actions. We will never be able to know whether human behavior is the product of necessity. Regardless of whether all events–including human actions–are caused, the issue of whether this determinism involves necessity (rather than probability) is metaphysical. In other words, we will never be able to resolve this issue on the basis of our observations. The world is too complex and open to too many reasonable interpretations to allow us to settle this issue scientifically. We do, however, want to believe that all events are caused, and most of us do want to believe that people are, to a large extent, free and responsible agents. To believe or act otherwise would be extremely difficult and depressing–if not psychologically impossible–for us.

What are the consequences of our believing and acting as if traditional determinism is false? Do we have to give up our belief that nature is uniform, that laws of nature are discoverable or that all events are caused? No. We are free to conceive of natural regularities as probabilistic, hence preserving an orderly world view. Furthermore, we are able, in good conscience, to retain our views that all human behavior is caused *and* that we are free and responsible agents. What are the consequences of our believing and acting as if traditional determinism is true? We can retain our faith in universal causation and orderliness, but we may well lose our ability to believe and act, in good conscience, as if we are free and responsible agents. This loss is bound to be deeply disturbing to most of us and would require radical revisions in our customs and institutions of responsibility. We stand to lose much that is significant to us if we believe and act as if traditional determinism is true. In the spirit of James' pragmatic philosophy, therefore, we are justified in believing and acting as if traditional determinism is false. Since traditional determinism has served as the only serious challenge to our belief that we are free and responsible agents, we are also pragmatically justified in continuing to believe and act as if we are such agents.

Five

WHAT IS RIGHT?

For several millennia philosophers have attempted to clarify the nature of morality. Like our familiarity with time, so too with moral right and wrong: we seem to understand it quite well until we try to explain it. What do we mean when we judge that something is "morally wrong"? What basis (standard or criteria) do we have for making such judgments? Is it the way we were raised, the customs of our society, God's will, or perhaps our subjective feelings? Furthermore, why should we act morally? Is it because we will be punished if we don't, either by others or God? Is it somehow in our overall self-interest to act morally? Will doing so make us happier than if we did not? Is the best reason for acting morally that such action is intrinsically worthwhile, whether or not our self-interest is served? In this final chapter, I will review standard answers to these questions and offer my own perspective.

1. Morality and Religion

One ancient and influential view is that moral good and evil is determined by the divine will. Consider as an example the Judeo-Christian heritage. Moses brought his tablets for the Jews to obey. The Ten Commandments were offered as the rock of morality, and their final authority was supposed to rest on the will of God.

What are we to do when the only choice left us means we must violate one or more of the Commandments? What if I must steal in order to show love for my starving family? What if I must kill in order to save the life of the mother or her unborn child (where one must perish if the other is to survive)? The Old Testament is unclear about how we are to decide such fairly common cases. We need a basic ethical principle which will simplify and bring an ordering to the complexity and conflicts of value we face in the world. For example, the Old Testament could have said (but does not) that the moral bottom-line is to avoid injuring people where possible, and, when not possible, to minimize the injury.

In the New Testament, Jesus does offer us moral counsel. This includes: turn the other cheek if someone harms you, and help other people, especially those who are suffering and underprivileged. He tells his disciples that if they cannot remember all of the Biblical rules, two commandments summarize the collective meaning of the rest:[1] love God, and love your neighbor as yourself. These top two Commandments serve, then, as the moral bottom-line. In any event, we can consider the Ten Commandments, or Jesus' top two, as more specific ways of pointing out what is harmful and what is beneficial for us. So the Bible does offer us principles for simplifying our moral insight, although it is silent on what we should do when we cannot avoid violating the rules laid down.

2. Philosophers' Views of Morality

We may classify traditional philosophical theories of morality according to four themes: Duty, Utility, Human Rights, and Self-Development. For the moment, I shall ignore theories that claim morality is culturally relative, purely subjective, or emotional. The duty-centered approach is called "deontology" and anchors moral right in fulfilling our obligations. Traditional religious codes of ethics (Christian, Moslem, or Hebrew) are examples of such an approach. The best-known example of deontology among philosophers was developed by Kant. According to one version of his categorical imperative, each of us should always act in such a way that we treat others as an end in themselves rather than simply as a means to our ends. In other words, when our actions will affect others, we should not act exclusively for manipulative or self-serving purposes. To be used (while not being respected as an end) by others is demeaning to our sense of dignity and self-worth–a fundamental harm which Kant proscribed by the adoption of the categorical imperative (which I will examine later). This way of proscribing selfish behavior (and favoring a world in which no one acts selfishly) would be a benefit to us all.

The utility-centered approach is called "utilitarianism" and was formulated by Jeremy Bentham and John Stuart Mill.[2] On this view, moral right amounts to maximizing the useful consequences of actions, institutions, and rules. The useful (utility) is measured in terms of what promotes pleasure or happiness. Negative utility amounts to pain or misery. We are to consider equally everyone who is affected, and our ideal is to produce a sum total balance of happiness over misery. Utilitarianism prohibits us from playing favorites with our friends, loved ones, community, nation, or ourselves. Even if we disagree that harm equals pain or misery, utilitarians aim for a world in which harm is minimized and benefit is maximized. Even where pain leads to (and is often essential for) a significant benefit, there is still something harmful about pain. Likewise, even where pleasure comes from or leads to a significant evil, there is something good about pleasure. This we can call the intrinsic good of pleasure and the intrinsic evil of pain.

Another classical approach to ethics holds that morality is to be rooted in respect for fundamental human rights. Champions of this view include Locke[3] and Rousseau.[4] The concept of basic human rights can be understood to flow from what each of us deserves in virtue of our having been created in the Divine likeness. Thus, each human being is conceived as equal from the point of view of the Creator. Basic human rights can also be understood as logically extending to everyone what we would (and rationally could) desire for ourselves. Thus, since each of us desires personal freedom, it is only natural to acknowledge the legitimacy of others' aspiration to the same. If we insist on something for ourselves, it seems arbitrary and unfair to deny that others should have it as well. There is an exception. If it is something that only one person *can*, given that person's unique circumstances, rationally insist on for herself or himself, then that person's attitude is not arbitrary or unfair. For example, so long as I live, no one but me has a right to have my heart.

Theorists of human rights typically rest the concept of our entitlements on our natural equality as human beings. This does not mean we are equal in physical or mental abilities;[4] we clearly are not. Instead, we are all equal in the need for food, warmth, shelter, etc. (our survival needs). We are all in need (as Locke suggests) of life and the liberty to pursue our own happiness. The only reasonable way to protect our ability to pursue our vital interests is to extend a guaranteed protection to everyone. We are also supposed equal before God. This means each of us is created in the divine image (with a soul), hence equally precious and equally obliged to honor the divine law.

Some emphasize the theme of realizing each person's self-potential. This secular approach is similar to the human rights approach save that it places no fundamental (if any) emphasis on the concept of human rights. Plato and Aristotle are classic examples of this approach. Even if someone believes in God (as Plato did), no mention is made of our having been "endowed by the

Creator with certain inalienable rights." We could include under this heading the natural law theology which is most highly developed within the Catholic tradition.[5] I choose not to classify it in this way because the natural law defines a person's potential with reference to God's will and God's intentions for us. This means that ultimately what a person should do is based super-naturally on obedience to God's will. Consequently, what we should do is understood in terms of our obligations to God. For this reason, the natural law tradition belongs more appropriately under the heading of deontology.

The goal of moral action is understood as the promotion of our full development as persons. Every living thing goes through a process, from birth to death, of growth-maturity-decay. The stage of maturity is viewed as the norm–the good–for each species. According to Plato and Aristotle, our human good involves the development of our rational capability for knowledge, deliberation, and self-control. For Plato human happiness and justice depends on our being in a condition where our knowledge of what is best controls the expression of our emotions and (non-rational) basic drives. As formulated in the *Republic*, you are considered just when your soul is in a balanced or harmonious condition so that each basic element of your soul is "minding its own business." This means that your reason must rule your non-rational elements. The non-rational includes your emotions, your dreams and fantasies, and your survival drives. Your rational elements include your ability to deliberate, to act contrary to your non-rational impulses, and your knowledge of what is best for you. When reason governs emotion and other non-rational drives, Plato believes the blind are led by what has insight and direction. Thus, just persons are conceived as "having it together," as having "their own house in order." By analogy, a society is considered just when it is ruled by those who are naturally best suited (because of their wisdom and noble intentions, not their power, cunning, or wealth) to rule. Plato believed such rulers would be lovers of philosophy. For Aristotle the good of human action is choosing a moderate course of action (between the extremes of excess and deficiency). The golden mean, for example, with regard to judging when it is right to kill would fall somewhere between never killing anything and killing whenever you felt like it. Obviously, either extreme threatens human well-being.[6]

Aside from our development as members of our species (humankind), the nurturing of our individuality is also vital. We should do what contributes to the complete flourishing of our natural talents as individual members of *homo sapiens*. This approach aims to promote human benefit and to discourage human injury. Benefit is conceived as whatever enhances our mature development. Injury is conceived as whatever blocks or stunts self-realization.

3. Problems With These Views

I argue for an amendment to the self-realization theory, which selects justice as the central theme of ethics. I emphasize "central theme" because I do not maintain that justice is the only consideration relevant to morality. Our obligations, following rules, respecting human rights, developing our self-potential, and the overall consequences for human happiness are all relevant to the quilt of morality. Justice, however, remains the central theme of morality because none of the above can determine what is right unless it is underwritten by considerations of justice. While the legal tradition maintains that justice is blind, I would maintain that all other moral standards are blind unless guided by justice.

What is inadequate about the rule or commandment-guided ethics of religion? To begin with, it requires faith, which agnostics and atheists do not have. Atheists and agnostics believe in a moral code by which they hope to live. If a precondition of this is that they must accept their code as bonafide only if they have faith in God, then they are excluded from the Moral Community. This I want to resist for several reasons.

First, according to Judaism, Christianity, and Islam, there is but one Creator, and we are all created in the image of this Creator. Since it is absurd to interpret this article of faith as implying that God has male or female genitalia (even the Bible is quite vague on how the union between the Holy Ghost and Mary was consummated), it is silly to think we are like God in so far as we are embodied beings, much less in virtue of being male or female in sex. I assume this "likeness" must refer to our having autonomous minds and wills, hence that believers, agnostics, and atheists are all like the Divine in their ability to think and to discriminate good from evil. This requires us to interpret the meaning of the Commandments. Does "Thou shall not kill" mean that we should not kill even in legitimate self-defense, that we should not kill any living thing, or what? If we adopt the translation, "Thou shall not murder," as some do, a similar quandary arises. Which acts of killing are unwarranted, hence murderous? I do not think it is hopeless for us to know how to answer such questions, and I do not believe God would create us with the inability to find our way to such answers. In the same vein, we need to be able to rank priorities when an action will bring the Commandments into conflict with one another. We may be faced with a situation where what we do will either violate the Commandment to honor our parents or the Commandment against stealing. Suppose our parents order us to steal something (which also will likely conflict with "Love Thy Neighbor"). In such difficult circumstances of choice, I cannot believe that we are supposed to have no reasonable hope of doing the right thing. But if I am correct, this is because we–including atheists and agnostics–are endowed with the ability to decide which is the lesser of the evils confronting us. The Catholic philosopher Aquinas would have called this "the natural light of reason," which he conceived as a gift to us from God. Thus, whether we are believers, atheists, or agnostics, this does not preclude us from having moral insight. At most, the creeds of Judaism, Christianity, and Islam would imply that the atheist or agnostic has one moral blind spot (a major one to be sure): non-believers "choose" not to believe that God exists.

The second reason for resisting the claim that only "true believers" can have moral insight concerns the relationship between God's will and morality. As I argued in Chapter Two, the question remains: Is something right because God wills it, or does God will it because it is right? If we accept the first alternative, morality is conceived as fundamentally based on power. Since God has the most power (including Will power), we who are far weaker should do what the strongest commands us to do. Also, on this view God invents moral standards rather than knows them. Since this view encourages an authoritarian paradigm of religion and values, it is dangerous. It can be appropriate to tell a child that he or she ought to do something because the parent (who is wiser) says so, but this is often inappropriate as a justification from one adult to another. An alternative way of conceiving of God is consistent with a reverent view of God and avoids authoritarianism. On this view, God wills us to behave in ways specified in the Ten Commandments because God, being all-knowing, knows what is moral and being all-loving, wills what is best for us. This being the case, God's Commandments are worthy of being followed not because God is Supreme Dictator of the Universe, but because God is benevolent and wise. Our knowledge and goodness being imperfect, we are wise to pay heed to God's will for us.

This paradigm of the Divine would not preclude the atheist or agnostic from moral insight. The atheist or agnostic need only have faith in morality (not in God also) in order to have moral insight. Since I know of no compelling reason to believe that God invents rather than knows what is right, I want believers to embrace a non-authoritarian view of God.

Finally, conceiving of ourselves as autonomous is crucial to any fully meaningful Christian, Judaic, or Islamic faith. This autonomy is critically damaged if we are denied the independent ability to judge good from bad, right from wrong. I refer here not only to the religious tradition which holds that we have free will and are accountable for choosing for or against God, but also to our ability to judge reliably what is from God, from human beings, or from Satan. If God is supposed not to have endowed us with a basic knowledge of good and bad, we are wholly unable to discern whether it is good to follow God's will. Indeed, we would be unable to reliably tell whether it is more worthy to follow God or Satan, not knowing which is good and which is bad. The whole notion of personal choice and responsibility for sin becomes meaningless unless we are granted some independent moral knowledge of what is right and wrong. Again, this means that moral knowledge is not the exclusive possession of the religious. This also means morality must be something more than obeying rules or commandments.

4. Deontology

Religious moral codes are typically examples of deontology–codes based on duty and obeying the rules. Although all of us (especially children) need rules of thumb to live by, I cannot accept the deontological approach. Where such approaches involve a list of rules or commands, several problems arise. To begin with, if our conception of acting morally is wed to following a list of specific rules, we are encouraged to embrace a mindset of blind obedience. This is stupid and insensitive. I imagine that Jesus meant to avoid this danger by simplifying all specific Jewish moral rules into two general ones. Nothing is noble about obedience; we must know what is worthy of being obeyed. Unless we have that knowledge, the result is slavery or sadomasochism. But to have such knowledge, we need to know something more than the rules. Another problem typical of deontology arises when we consider the conflicts that can arise among the specific rules we are to obey. If one of these rules is supposed to have priority, then it is not obedience to the rules which is moral, but obeying the more important rule. The key here would lie in our knowing why some rules take precedence over others. Otherwise, the most we could know is the hollow generality, "Follow the rule which takes precedence," without knowing when or how it is to be applied.

One deontological approach that avoids this problem is proposed by Kant.[7] He argued that we are obliged to follow only one rule–the categorical imperative. One of the ways he formulated this imperative is as follows: Act on that rule of action which you can will as a universal rule of action. For example, should I lie to my friend David about the reason I missed our lunch date? If the rule of action (Kant speaks of "maxims") here is "I will tell a lie," I need to consider whether I would be willing for everyone to act on such a principle. It is dangerous for me when others deceive me, and certainly I would not be willing to have such deception occur all the time. Nevertheless, it is not clear whether the rule of action concerns lying always, mostly, occasionally, or rarely. A person trying to determine his or her duty in this case might well be unsure whether "the" action could be willed as a universal rule, thereby remaining unsure of what to do.

This problem illustrates another difficulty for "universalizability" as a principle of decision. When we consider generalizing a rule of action from a concrete circumstance, which generalization should we pick? For example, should I lie to David about the reason I missed our lunch appointment? Kant would have us next consider whether I can will my rule of action as a universal law of action. Fine, but how should I generalize this? Kant did not consider this a problem. Each of the following (and many more) rules could be picked:

R1: Everyone will lie to others and to themselves.
R2: Everyone will lie to others.
R3: Everyone will lie to strangers.
R4: Everyone will lie to their friends.
R5: Everyone will lie to their close friends.
R6: Everyone will lie to their close friends about their reasons for missing appointments with them.

If R1-R6 mean that everyone sometimes does such a thing, I might well be willing to accept such a consequence, supposing I have in mind "white lies" or lies which prevent a far greater evil. Still this may not be morally relevant to the kind of lie or circumstances I confront concretely. In short, the meaning of Kant's categorical imperative is excessively vague. As it stands, we could choose a description of the act under consideration which, when generalized, allowed us to rationalize what we were already predisposed to do–regardless of morality.

I find all theories of moral right and wrong are bound (unless wholly implausible on other grounds) to be more vague than we would like them to be. No moral theory will rule out any possibility of being abused or misapplied through human rationalization or error. My main objection to Kant's duty-centered ethics is the same as my objection to founding ethics on obeying religious rules. Such an approach fosters blind obedience and authoritarianism. The hazard of this from Kant's approach may be greater since the only clear counsel we have is to obey "the categorical imperative," to do our "duty," without having a clear enough notion of how to determine what that duty is.

5. Human Rights

For similar reasons, we should reject a view of ethics which bases morality on human rights if these are conceived as absolutes. In the same way that particular duties can conflict with one another, so too can particular human rights (and they can be construed as resting on the will of God). If we have a right to freedom and security (as I believe we do), this is because it benefits us to have a wide measure of both. It injures us to be enslaved or to be made insecure.

The concept of basic human rights is a positive development for moral consciousness. Millennia of human experience show us that people abuse one another in many ways–due to greed, fear, hatred, the corrupting influence of great power, and other excesses. Monarchs and powerful governments have a long record of abusing their citizens. Corporate greed and short-term thinking have all-too-often resulted in employee exploitation and environmental devastation. To the extent that morality seeks to promote the general welfare and to minimize suffering, we would be wise to insist that basic human rights need to be respected and enforced. We would also be wise to construe such rights as provisional or conditional. For example, we need to have human free expression protected, but this does not necessarily extend to yelling "Fire" in a crowded theater, to slander, or to liable. Absolute respect for a particular human right will tend to be abusive of some other human right. The basic human rights we recognize should be viewed as vital rules of thumb to be balanced against one another such that the burden of proof is always on the party who seeks to violate a particular right. It is also imperative that such rights truly reflect fundamental and healthy human needs. It won't do to have frivolous rights (the right to drive as fast as we like) or rights based on unhealthy or extremist motivations like hatred, greed, or compulsion. We would not be moral to guarantee the right to vengeance, to consume as many drugs as we desire, or to own as much as we can take possession of. Such consuming desire and greed inevitably interfere with others' legitimate needs and desires.

6. Utilitarianism

The main problem with utilitarianism is that moral good is defined in terms of pleasure or happiness without reference to fairness or justice. The only concession made to these key moral concepts lies in the principle that every person's happiness or misery counts equally. Thus, utilitarians are committed to the view that we should not play favorites in deciding how to maximize good (happiness or pleasure) over evil (misery or pain). While a step in the right direction, this yields an inadequate concept of justice. Suppose we can do something which produces a total of happiness over misery, but only by making a majority of people happy at the price of the cruel enslavement of a minority. Especially if the minority is quite small, this action would be judged moral according to utilitarianism, yet it would otherwise appear to be monstrously unjust. Utilitarians try to argue that such cases could never occur as a matter of fact (hence that their theory does satisfy the moral demand for justice and fair play), but their arguments are unconvincing. Because utilitarianism divorces happiness and misery from the issue of whether either is deserved, utilitarianism is destined to remain a highly suspect view of morality.

7. Self-Realization and Justice?[8]

The fourth approach to morality is based on self-realization. Long ago Plato and Aristotle argued that moral virtue is to be found in properly realizing ourselves as human beings. What is best for us (human excellence) is the same thing as justice and happiness of a certain kind. By living in a society which nurtures our ability to achieve excellence, and by choosing to strive for such excellence, we will naturally behave justly and achieve happiness. Such a view is correct, but problems arise if we are not careful in how we interpret the desirability of self-development. In particular, the good of self-realization must be filtered through the lenses of health, fairness, and justice. Unless these standards illuminate the concept of self-realization, the concept degenerates into anarchy, nihilism, egoism, or tyranny.

Suppose we said that moral right is the same thing as self-realization without any limitations of health, fairness, or justice. If so, then no matter how people "developed," their behavior would still count as moral. Thus, infantile actions, problem-drinking, other forms of drug addiction, rape, and murder would all be morally proper ways of realizing self-potential. But we can hardly consider such behavior desirable, whether on moral grounds or otherwise. Can we realize our potential through self-destructive and other-destructive anarchy? We want to distinguish self-development from expansive behavior *per se*, just as we want to distinguish normal growth from cancerous growth.

A "value-neutral" notion of self-development also amounts to an endorsement of egoism and tyranny. Suppose we do not assume that positive self-realization must involve fairness or justice. Instead, let us imagine that each of us is equally entitled to do whatever will enhance our self-development, even if that means, *carte blanche*, abusing or ignoring the self-interest of others. This will not mean that we should always ignore how we harm others–for we may want not to harm our friends and loved ones. Nor will this mean we should automatically choose to realize our goals at the expense of strangers. Harming others may cause us harm in return, thereby injuring our self-development. Instead, let us imagine that we should restrain our self-expression (to avoid injuring the self-development of others) only when we choose to or when harming them would also do significant damage to ourselves. If we choose to be considerate of others, we should act considerately. Likewise, if we want to do something which will harm someone else who is in no position to threaten our interests, we should do so.

Such a view of the "good" of self-realization endorses a world view according to which we are all competitors in a struggle for dominance. Those who are in a position to dominate others–by virtue of their physical, emotional, or mental strength–should do so in order to realize their potential. Put otherwise, so long as it is rationally guided, "might makes right." The weaker are also entitled to realize their potential; it's just that they have less potential than those who are stronger. Such an "unrestrained" notion of self-realization finds acceptable both selfishness and tyranny. I find such consequences unhealthy and immoral.

To act morally is to treat people justly, to give people the treatment they "deserve." What we deserve is only partly a matter of what we do to merit being punished or rewarded. Justice is more than retribution. Being just also refers us to what is best for us. Unless we have an understanding of what is good for individuals and for society, punishment becomes a cruel and arbitrary custom. Unless we presume that people deserve to have a good life–a healthy life–it is odd for us to be morally indignant when some people do damage to others' lives. If those who are harmed did not deserve to have what they lost, why should we hold the thief blameworthy for taking it? A vital function of justice is to protect and promote the good (healthy) life. The aim must be to enable people and society to be as healthy as possible. This we all deserve even if we do nothing to deserve it. Not everything we deserve must be earned by virtuous behavior. For example, if you pass a stranger on the street, you deserve to be treated with respect even though the stranger has no knowledge of whether you have done anything to deserve respect. Justice requires retribution, but when reward or punishment makes an individual or society–on balance–sicker, justice is not served.

This means we must treat each other with at least a minimal amount of loving care. Leaving aside for the moment the nature of a healthy human life, how are we to achieve this goal? None of us are inclined (whether by nature, society, or environment) always to behave in healthy ways. Infants need to be nurtured and disciplined; human development is social. Without the community of adult others, the human infant will not learn to behave healthily or to survive. Even as adults, we behave in ways that are unhealthy for ourselves and for others. We are sometimes intentionally cruel, and often we are cruel through negligence or indifference. We need a means of protecting our right to live in health: physical, emotional, and mental. If we deserve to live healthily, we also deserve a healthy means of protecting our health. This is the positive expression of the vengeful "an eye for an eye." If morality requires us to continually adjust the balance of good and evil, let us do so in a way that illuminates rather than obscures sight.

Supposing we all deserve to be as healthy as possible, how shall we treat people who injure others? How shall we treat people who injure the health of their community (and this includes the human family)? What is appropriate? What do they deserve? For example, what does the person deserve who steals public tax dollars? The thief must be held accountable for the theft. The rewards of theft are clear, and people learn in large measure by example. If the person who stole is not held accountable, the thief and anyone else has no incentive to avoid such temptations. This leads to the further breakdown of the community's health through a loss of public confidence in the government.

Shall we punish the thief? Would this not amount to vengeance and interfering with the thief's health? We should punish the thief, and this need not imply either of the above. Even though we need do nothing to deserve health, life, liberty, and the pursuit of happiness–we can do things to forfeit our full claim to these goods. As is done in medical practice, so we should inflict an injury on the thief in order to promote the health of the thief and of society. This is what we all deserve. We have three alternatives: (1) we can reward the thief's behavior, (2) penalize it, or (3) do nothing. If (1) or (3), we will be doing nothing to promote healthy behavior. By appropriately punishing the thief, the thief and others have an opportunity to learn from the thief's suffering. Human experience shows that we can often learn something positive from suffering. Suffering is not inherently and wholly negative or inhumane. Only some kinds of suffering are threats to our overall health: undeserved suffering, torture, and severe pain. In punishing people for immoral behavior, we must avoid cruel and unusual punishment, and we must keep our sight set on rehabilitation whenever feasible. Punishment and rehabilitation are not necessarily in opposition to one another. It is healthy for each of us and society at large to appreciate the injuries we do to people. Unless we suffer for the injury we do others, this lesson will not be taken to heart. Our suffering makes us focus on the cause of our sad condition, or makes us ask why we are suffering.

Appropriate moral punishment focuses our attention on our role in causing injury as well as someone else's disapproval of that action. In effect, a typical result of being punished is that we are made aware of our responsibility for the suffering we face. Do we want to be the sort of person who would ever again do such a thing? Do we accept our having played a meaningful role in wrongfully harming someone? Are we willing to risk being punished like this again? If not, then we have an incentive to reform. We deserve to live healthy lives, and the best way to heal ourselves of unhealthy behavior is by accepting personal responsibility for that behavior. Being blamed, criticized, chastised, or punished for such behavior is the best way for us to accept such responsibility. We are due this because the entire community needs an efficient means of discouraging unhealthy behavior. This is the positive meaning of retribution.

This does not mean that we can appreciate the loss we have caused another only by being made to suffer as much as they did. This point can be illustrated in several ways. First, the logic of an "eye for an eye" is absurd. If we have unjustly harmed someone else, then the only way we can suffer an equal injury is if we are also made to suffer an equally unjust injury. Other things being equal, unjust suffering is always worse than suffering *per se*. But we should never do what is the more unjust of several alternatives. By responding to one injustice with another one, we are only doubling the amount of injustice done–thereby choosing to create more rather than less injustice. If we were truly to follow the "eye for an eye" maxim in cases of responding to unjust actions, we would need to excessively punish the moral violator or punish another innocent person (perhaps a loved one of the violator). Or in the case where the injustice involved one person inadequately compensating another, we would need to inadequately compensate the violator–say by rewarding a murderer or by a sentence of a $20 fine. Surely, the illogic of this illustrates the blinding influence of an "eye for an eye."

We can make this point in another way. The person who acts unjustly creates an unhealthy state of affairs. If we respond in kind (as we often do), we also thereby create an unhealthy state of affairs–again adding to rather than healing the injury to individuals and society.[9] We are supposed to be teaching someone a lesson, meant to prevent the transgressor or others from such threatening behavior. But we can quite reasonably wonder which lesson we communicate by this practice. Consider the case of capital punishment. A person is duly tried and convicted of murder, sentenced to die, then executed by the State. Supposing the person really was guilty, he or she will surely be prevented from ever again committing murder. This, however, is the only clear consequence of this action by the State. Many others in society–including friends, loved ones, and those prone to resolve conflicts through violence–may well see the lesson here in one of the following ways. (1) If someone kills someone, you are entitled to kill that person. (2) If someone commits a severe injustice against you, you are entitled to commit a severe injustice against that person. (3) If you are powerful enough to enforce your will and desire revenge or to set an example, then you are entitled to do so. It will be futile to respond that none of these is our intended message. People know all-too-well that we may not understand our true motive for action, or we may not truthfully report that motive. People will arrive at the interpretation which makes the most sense to them. The old saying is: "The road to hell is paved with good intentions."

If many people do interpret "the lesson" of capital punishment as (1)-(3), this is not a healthy consequence for society. If (1) is the lesson learned, the executioner and those who authorize the execution should also be killed. If (2) is the lesson, then those who feel that the execution was a severe injustice against them (and their lost loved one) will infer that they should commit a grave injustice against the authorities who executed their loved one. If (3) is the lesson then people will become cynical about the criminal justice system and hope to gain enough power so that they are entitled to extract their "pound of flesh." Such lessons learned are damaging to the integrity of society.

Though deterrence is an important goal of punishment, so too is justice. Morally speaking, this means that our deterrent strategy should be just. Contrary to utilitarianism, we cannot allow the noble goal of promoting the general welfare or the public good to be decisive in determining our response to moral wrongdoing. We cannot, for example, condone punishing innocent people (while concealing their innocence) in order to deter others. Consider the offense of murder. No one deserves to be murdered, and society deserves to be protected from murder. Suppose a well-beloved public figure is murdered, and the public cries out for justice to be done. An unscrupulous district attorney might decide to prosecute an innocent person in order to quiet the public outrage and deter others from murder. A drifter, or homeless person, a porn bookstore owner (or anyone considered suspicious or undesirable by the public) could be selected as the scapegoat. So long as the evidence was sufficient to persuade a jury to deliver a conviction and a harsh sentence, this punishment could be just as effective as punishing the guilty person.

Such a response would be a parody of justice. Society deserves to be protected from the wrongdoing, but only insofar as wrongdoers commit such offenses. It is the murderer and rapist we need protection from–not the abstractions of murder and rape. To reject this would be to savagely undercut the distinction between the value of the end and the value of the means. If the end justified any effective means to bring about that end, we could execute adults and children for lying, petty theft, etc.–since we can be quite confident that such punishment will prevent the person executed from ever again committing such an offense.

Some people may wonder whether justice can play the supreme role in moral decision-making that I am suggesting. We could find ourselves in the following dilemma: punish an innocent person, or many equally innocent people will suffer an even greater injustice! In such a case, wouldn't the morally right thing be to choose the lesser of two evils: punish the innocent person? Can't we conceive of cases involving vengeful nuclear extortionists which would require such a choice?

We probably can imagine such possible circumstances, albeit they are exceptionally unlikely to be faced by us in the real world. Given the circumstances of moral choice we are likely to confront in our lives, it will be most improbable that a causal link exists between our punishing an innocent person and the elimination of a graver injustice. Still, it could happen. What should we do in the sad event that it does? Some might maintain we should refrain from punishing the innocent person on the assumption that refraining from committing injustice is morally preferable to committing injustice (sins of omission versus sins of commission). On the other hand, you can choose not to commit this injustice, and thereby allow (but not cause) other forces to bring about a greater injustice. The upshot here would be that the moral imperative is to concentrate on the injustice you would be responsible for causing.

Perhaps such reasoning is sound, but I cannot accept it. I think we are morally obliged to do (or avoid doing) whatever we are reasonably sure will minimize injustice. The other stance is too purist and rests on too narrow a conception of moral responsibility. Therefore, I concede that cases may arise where we would be morally obliged to punish or otherwise knowingly injure innocent people. I speak of dreadful circumstances in which no matter what we do (or don't do), our choice will contribute to the existence of an injustice. In such cases we should choose the lesser of the two evils. But this concession provides no endorsement of any general practice of punishing the innocent in order to protect the public against wrongdoing. A few considerations weigh against such a conclusion. One, I doubt that most citizens would feel safer or be safer if they knew people were deliberately being punished for offenses committed by others. Two, it will be difficult to reasonably establish that punishing innocents will actually alleviate a greater injustice. Three, such an unjust practice–if condoned–will threaten the security of the general public. Given our high rate of violent crime and the normal career ambitions of public prosecutors, the next innocent person punished could be any one of us.

8. Being Fair and Being Just

Being fair is not equal treatment (in an unqualified sense). Treating everyone equally would be unfair in the extreme. We can hardly act fairly if we treat the innocent and the guilty alike, or treat the shoplifter as we treat the murderer. In order to be fair, we must, oddly enough, acknowledge and respect inequality–treating like cases alike and dissimilar cases differently. Neither is fairness the same thing as following the Golden Rule. According to the Golden Rule, we ought to treat others as we would be willing to be treated, but what if we have a low regard for ourselves? What if we accept self-neglect or abuse and are alcoholic, anorexic, a compulsive gambler, a victim of child abuse, etc.? If people have an excessively low self-image (and there are many such people), they may believe that they deserve to be treated poorly, and according to the Golden Rule, they would be justified, therefore, in their ill treatment of others. But this is not fair to others or themselves. We must not confound equal treatment with fair treatment.

The person who acts justly and the person who acts unjustly do not deserve equal treatment. Those who act justly show through example how we should behave; they teach a lesson. Those who act unjustly show us that they need to be taught a lesson. Both the innocent and the guilty deserve to lead healthy lives, but the path to health is different in each case. Just as pain is a natural warning that our physical or mental health is endangered by something, so too the moral violator should receive the discomforting message that something is wrong and is in need of a remedy. Whether from others or from our own conscience, this is the minimal function of moral chastisement or punishment. We are given a "wake up call" that something is seriously wrong with our attitudes or behavior.

Morality requires that all persons be afforded respect, but the kind of respect appropriate to the innocent is different from that appropriate to the transgressor. In the case of the transgressor, we criticize or punish the offender out of respect for others' health and for an ideal of human behavior. It is an error to think that the discomfort caused by moral censure implies lack of respect for the person who is censured. This may often be the attitude of people who chastise others for wrongdoing, but this should be no reflection on the general practice of moral disapproval. No more does a physician show disrespect for a patient by a diagnosis which the patient finds unsettling. The overriding concern is to assist the patient back to health, and to protect the community from any illness which the patient might otherwise spread. In the case of moral criticism or censure, all normally sensitive people are like the physician. Here, the saying, "Physician heal thyself," means that none of us are immune from moral criticism or censure. It also means we should judge ourselves as surely and swiftly as we would judge others.

To approximate fairness, we must supplement, "Treat others as you would want to be treated," with "Treat yourself well." Nevertheless, the Golden Rule is useful as a red flag to keep us wary of the possibility that we are using a double-standard in our treatment of others. If we find we are treating others in ways we would not be willing to be treated, we had better be sure we have sufficient reason to justify this double-standard. Otherwise, we are acting hypocritically and insensitively. It will never suffice to "justify" such a double-standard for us to say, "Well, they are not me; I am unique." This reasoning is silly and unconvincing. It is silly because each person is "unique" or not exactly alike anyone else. But if each of us is unique in this sense, then paradoxically we are all exactly alike in this way; hence, our uniqueness can no longer be a difference which makes our case special. Our "specialness" will be no more special than anyone else's. Rationalizing our poor treatment of others along these lines will give the appearance of thinly-veiled selfishness and childishness.

If fairness is an essential guideline to helping people realize their self-potential, what is justice? Sometimes we speak of fairness as justice, but we might do better to speak of them as separate and distinct concepts. Being fair implies giving someone what they (minimally) deserve, but we also deserve (according to justice) to be treated fairly. If I treat all my family impartially by treating them all equally poorly, then I am treating them fairly in a sense. But, though I am impartially distributing poor treatment to them, I am not treating them justly. One of the things we deserve is to be treated fairly, but we deserve more than this. We should think of justice (rather than fairness) as covering the totality of what we deserve. In order to be just, we have to be fair, but we can be fair without being just.

9. Which Is More Just?

In the same way that not all suffering is morally wrong, but only unnecessary or unjustified suffering, so too we cannot say that injustice is always wrong. It would be wonderful if we could avoid harming or being unjust to anyone in our lives. As it happens, the world does not permit this luxury. Some kinds of injury are inevitable, and so are some instances of unfairness. In order to become our own persons, we have to be weaned from our parents. This process of separation is traumatic. In order to be healed or protected from illness, we often have to accept some minor injury, a shot in the arm or surgery. Sometimes our friendship requires us to tell our friends unpleasant truths. Likewise, we are sometimes in circumstances where, no matter what we do, we will be unfair to someone. Odd as it may sound, putting a person who is guilty of assault or rape in jail is not fair to his or her loved ones. They typically will suffer from the loss and yet have done nothing to deserve this suffering. But failing to put the guilty party in jail would be even more unfair to the victim and to society. Unless we are opposed to all forms of punishment, we believe that a person who commits a moral crime of violence deserves to be appropriately punished. Failing to administer such punishment is itself unfair. We have to choose the lesser evil, the lesser injustice.

10. Health

I have said that promoting health is a vital aim of justice. But what is health? How can morality be centered on such an emotionally laden and vague concept? Aside from clear-cut examples from medicine concerning our bodily health, don't judgments about health tell us more about the attitudes of the judger than they do about any genuine features of human beings or their behavior? Attempting to clarify the nature of moral right by appeal to the concept of healthy development may introduce more darkness than light on the subject.

While I admit that the concept of health contains vagueness, and while I would concede that the application of this concept can be abusive (where a person is certified mentally ill for political or ideological reasons), I think this concept is clear enough and stable enough to help explain the nature of justice. For example, we know (if we know anything) that we cannot be healthy unless our survival needs are met. People who are malnourished or who lack adequate shelter will be unhealthy. Thus, people who desire the conditions to assure their survival have healthy attitudes, and to the extent they choose to behave in ways appropriate to sustain these conditions, their actions are healthy. Severe prolonged pain invades our consciousness, immobilizes us to a great extent, and hampers or blocks our ability to function. Consequently, such pain is unhealthy. Yet many types of pain, even severe pain, have a healthy side. Pain informs us that something is wrong, and thus is a signal for us to locate the cause of the pain and cope with that cause in an appropriate way. Attempting to ignore, minimize, or eliminate pain without focusing on the source of the pain can be unhealthy. If an athlete has a slight bone fracture in his or her leg and continues to run on it, for example, by deadening the pain with drugs, this effort to "play through the injury" may result in a severely broken leg.

Beyond our survival needs and our need to cope with pain in a healthy way, we need some freedom and we need to be loved and appreciated. Without these, we are unhappy, and an unhappy human being is not well. When we have our survival needs met, but have little freedom and feel unloved, we are, as the saying goes, merely existing. Finally, we need problems, obstacles, and challenges. Without obstacles to overcome and without problems to cope with, we cease to grow, and instead stagnate. When a person views marriage as an end to striving, as automatic bliss, unhappiness will follow. When a person views retirement in the same way, the disappointment will be great. We don't need problems that overwhelm and crush us, but we do need problems to maintain our sense of well-being. As it is, we need not worry that this condition of happiness will be denied us. There is little prospect that life will take away our obstacles and problems.

As an extension of our individual selves and as a means to protect our individual vulnerability, society will be healthy to the extent that its customs and institutions promote rather than detract from human health. Thus, a society which finds few ways to protect the conditions necessary for healthy individual development will be a quite unhealthy society. Socrates likened our society to our parents,[10] but this is not quite right. Society is a hybrid of a parent and an offspring. It is like a parent insofar as its laws and institutions provide for our nurture (through schools, police, and fire protection), and insofar as it exists before us and typically after us. But it is also a human creation that cannot exist without our nurture and support. This constitutes the basis for the good citizen: the person who fully realizes the symbiotic relationship between personal health and the health of society.

11. The Basis of Morality

Philosophers have long debated whether moral judgments reflected anything objective about the world, and if so, whether moral standards were universal or relative in their scope. They have also debated whether being moral is in our self-interest or whether the most we could claim is that being moral is good for its own sake. Discussing these issues will be my last project.

Since G.E. Moore's *Principia Ethica*[11] and David Hume's *Treatise of Human Nature*[12] some philosophers have thought it was a fundamental confusion to identify moral good with natural states of affairs. Moore argued it was a fallacy to identify goodness with any natural property (say, pleasure). No matter what natural feature we might equate with the good, Moore argued we could still meaningfully ask, "But is this good?" He called this the "open-question test," and he believed it showed that goodness could not be defined in naturalistic terms. Indeed, Moore believed good to be a unique property which we intellectually intuit, but do not perceive in the world of nature. Hume argued that a logical abyss separates what *is* factually true from what *ought* to be true. He believed that our "moral thoughts" reflected sentiments and passions, especially our feeling of compassion for others' suffering. I am not persuaded that good cannot be what is natural, factual, or actual.

Moore's open-question test proves little if it proves anything. If it proves anything, it proves that judgments of identity where different terms (say, "pleasure" and "good") appear on either side of the "equation" are less obviously acceptable to us than cases where the same term appears on both sides. "Pleasure = good" is less obvious to us than "Good = good"! This fact hardly shows that good, or moral goodness, is not the same thing as something natural like pleasure or health. Suppose there are various natural states of affairs–pleasure, happiness, and health–each of which is a moral good. That we could not define moral good as any one of them would hardly show that moral goods are not natural states of affairs.

Neither is Hume's claim persuasive. It is true that we cannot always soundly infer what ought to be from what is actually the case. For example, the fact that murders occur all-too-often does not entitle us to conclude that murder is morally right. This hardly shows that we can never soundly infer "an ought from an is." John Searle has argued we can do this.[13] I find dubious the Humean premise that only pure facts and pure thoughts exist such that the one logically excludes the other. Why not include the following as examples of *evaluative facts*?

(1) Jacques having shot to death a clerk, who threatened him in no significant way while robbing the store, was wrong.
(2) Mary having beaten and hospitalized her one-year old daughter was wrong.
(3) President Bush having started a war in order to boost his popularity was wrong.

Such facts differ from non-evaluative facts like Jacques shot a clerk, Mary beat up her daughter, President Bush started a war. They also differ from murder is wrong, child abuse is immoral, and other more abstract evaluative facts that seem true by definition. Why should non-evaluative facts have top priority as facts, and why should it matter that we cannot derive evaluative facts from their non-evaluative cousins? If there are evaluative facts rather than "only" non-evaluative facts, then we can sometimes soundly infer what ought to be from what is. I know of no proof that all facts are "purely" descriptive, and until such a proof is given, we have no reason for denying the existence of natural moral goods and evils.

Do we discover moral good and evil by perceiving something in our world? If not, do we somehow discover such good and evil through our power of understanding and intelligence? Aristotle said yes to the first question. Moore and Kant said yes to the second question. Hume and Nietzsche, have said no to both questions, arguing instead that morality is emotive or invented. In the twentieth century, philosophers on the whole have been skeptical that moral good and evil are discovered by us, especially if this means moral qualities exist in the world. Instead, many have construed moral judgments as subjective, emotive, or culturally relative. Something substantial is at issue here. The more we view a concept as derived from a reality independent of personal belief and perception, the more inclined we are to take seriously judgments involving that concept. This is especially true regarding our attitude toward others when their judgments contradict our judgment. If our concept of morality reflects a standard independent of any of our beliefs or perceptions, then our moral judgments can be correct or incorrect. Supposing this is so, that standard is either binding only within the framework of our culture, or its applicability is not confined to any particular culture. If a moral standard is not confined in application to a particular culture, we have good reason to believe that there is a universal (non-relativistic) basis for morality.

Let us suppose for the sake of argument that no independent standards of moral right and wrong exist, and that these standards are culturally relative. When in Iran, do as the Shia Moslems do; when in America, do as the Americans do. Under this relativistic theory of morality, moral truth will not be in the eyes of the beholder. When our perceptions or beliefs are at odds with customs of our culture, our perceptions or beliefs will simply be mistaken. Moral right and wrong would not be subjective, determined by individual preferences, emotions, or perspectives. If a woman in Iran judges it is morally okay for her to wear a short dress in public, she will be mistaken. If a woman in the United States believes it is immoral for any American woman to wear a short dress in public, she will also be mistaken. When cultural customs concerning right and wrong "contradict" one another, neither culture will be in error. If a conflict arises between two cultures over their divergent standards, say about women's dress, neither can presume that its standard is rationally entitled to prevail over the other. Their disagreement reveals a power struggle. Whose will-power should prevail? To resolve the dispute rationally, only the following sorts of issues will be appropriate. Are the consequences of "fighting" (the exact form of the struggle can vary) to impose our customs on the other worth it? Would it be more prudent to concede, to compromise, or to agree to disagree? Whatever we decide, the bottom-line will be power and cultural egoism. It will be pointless for either side to try to convince the other that its customs are more (or less) based on moral fact.

The reasons for resisting such a culturally relative theory of morality are similar to those for resisting moral subjectivism. In the case of subjectivism, no one's attitudes about what is right or wrong can be correct or incorrect. All moral disputes between people will merely reflect individual preferences, and resolving them will only amount to who is willing to concede power (and to what extent) and who is not. The Charlie Manson or Adolf Hitler perspectives will be every bit as legitimate as anyone else's. In the case of cultural relativism, it will not be the individual who is elevated beyond rational criticism, but the customs of one's culture. All moral disagreements *between* cultures in their origin and resolution can only be a matter of "pure" politics. If you hope for a kinder and gentler world community, as I do, this prospect is depressing.

Consider a world (not unlike ours) in which the intellectual conscience of all nations informs them that the only appropriate basis for resolving moral disputes between nations is power and calculations of self-interest. "What is a just way of resolving such conflicts?" will be an anachronistic and pointless question. In *The Republic*, Thrasymachus argues that justice (if it is to be a virtue) is the interest of the stronger party. When a vastly stronger nation comes into "moral" conflict with a weak nation, why should the stronger nation not seek to impose its perspective (way of life) on the weaker? It can do so in good conscience without fearing it might be violating any moral common ground (of justice) shared with the weaker culture. The stronger party has no reason to doubt that its standard of justice might in any way be misguided. "Might makes right" has always been tempting for the strong–regardless of the nature of justice. Under the present hypothesis, it will be more than a temptation, it will be beyond rational criticism so long as a nation correctly judges that its interest is to impose its will on other nations. I do not desire to endorse any view which lends blanket support to cultural imperialism. Such arrogance and cruelty were bad enough when carried out under the guise of God and absolutism. It will be no improvement that they can be justified under the banner of cultural relativism.

The loss of perceived common ground is something to be feared. So long as we believe we share some core value-commitments with an adversary, we realize that we have a basis for compromise and are inclined to temper our response to the conflict. If we view an adversary as a barbarian from a culture which is wholly lacking in "civilized values," we will have little if any compassion for the other's perspective. The adversary becomes the wholly other, the sub-human, the enemy. Once we have dehumanized our adversary, we have little reason to moderate our way of coping with such an alien form of life. Before we begin to conquer or kill the Alien, we think them to death. This does not mean we will necessarily act temperately with those with whom we feel close to, family or loved ones. Crimes of hate committed against those we love are all-too-common. What it does mean is that the more alien we view others with whom we have a conflict, the less reason we have for being considerate of their values and practices. Absent a common ground of perceived common values, all manner of coercion, violence, and warfare will seem justified in resolving conflicts.

Logically speaking, the absence of any shared moral standard does not dictate intolerance. Tolerance of the difference would be equally justified, although tolerance of radical value differences would be the most natural response only if we already were committed to fairness as a moral value standard. The essential point is that given the emotional import for us of our moral values, many of us will not feel it important to respect the Alien's norms.

In summary, our accepted moral value standards are a vital part of our sense of personal (and social) identity. We tend strongly to be defensive (which can lead us to be quite aggressive) against any attack on our sense of self and community. One pragmatic reason for presupposing universally applicable moral standards is to maximize the scope of the perceived moral community. The more we view a conflict as arising within our moral community, as defined in large part by the value-framework we share with others, the more likely we are to see the conflict as one which can and should be resolved short of war, violence, or coercion. The desire to be maximally inclusive in regard to who belongs to the moral community motivates in large measure my resistance to moral subjectivism and moral relativism.

I propose that we construe justice as the best basis for assessing what is morally right. I also suggest that we view justice as an objective and non-culturally relative standard. I say "best" because our concept of right and wrong is not solely derived from our understanding of what is just or unjust. Moral teaching in societies proceeds initially by parents and other authorities insisting to children that they follow rules–"do's and don'ts." During our formative years, this is how our concept of morality is formed, and these emotion-laden do's and don'ts may remain with us for the rest of our lives. As we grow older, we hear more frequently that justice is paramount, but by this time we have developed a sense of right and wrong based on the "do's and don'ts" already taught us. At times we base our judgment of wrong on the basis that something is quite different from what we are familiar with. The Alien is threatening, and our sense of the familiar (even of our sense of personal identity) is largely formed by the moral valuations we learn from our parents' admonitions. No wonder, then, that we are so often repulsed by the different sexual preferences of other persons or by the strange customs of other cultures.

Still, we do come to understand that being just is vital to being moral. We not only judge the wrongness of behavior on the basis of adultery, lying, stealing, and murder, but also on the basis of injustice. We come to realize that justice can permit or require stealing, lying, and killing in some circumstances. Most of the moral "do's and don'ts" initially taught us are similar to one another in presuming the standard of justice. Stealing is typically taking from another what we do not deserve (and what the other does not deserve to lose). Lying is typically putting others at a disadvantage they do not deserve. Murdering another is likewise an undeserved theft (of life). Treating others with abuse or neglect is typically not the way we would "love" ourselves, hence is unfair and undeserved. Making love with another's spouse or making love with someone other than our spouse is typically a case of causing someone undeserved harm by breaking an agreement of fidelity. The standard of justice seems to unify and pervade the background of most of the moral rules we are taught. As we mature mentally and emotionally, justice plays an even more vital role in our understanding of what is morally right or wrong. The concept of justice plays an especially unifying and simplifying role in our sense of priorities. The only case in which it is not wrong to act unjustly is when we have no choice, in which case we should commit the lesser injustice. For these reasons, the standard of justice appears the best candidate for maximizing membership in the moral community.

12. Is Morality Subjective or Relative?

Wishful thinking aside, some thinkers may wonder whether we can really treat justice and moral right as fully objective concepts. Can we conceive of them as on a par with the objectivity of perceptual, scientific, or mathematical judgments? Can what is just be compared with what is yellow, six inches wide, or travels 96,000 m.p.h.?

I see no overwhelming reason for answering "no" to these questions. As a value standard, we can think of justice and other moral values as being as objective as the value-standards of truth, knowledge, logical validity, consistency, and scientific method. When we judge that something is true, known, valid, consistent, or scientifically confirmed, we suppose our judgment reflects a state of affairs independent of our beliefs, likes and dislikes. We can attribute this objectivity to our concept of justice. Any of us can mistakenly judge that something is right or just (with the exception of judgments like "Justice is justice"). Not being infallible in our judgment about something implies (if there is *any* truth about the subject) the independence and objectivity of what is judged.

Three general reasons exist why people have doubted the objectivity and constancy of moral value. One is the fact that moral judgments are laced with emotions as well as pro and con attitudes. This reveals human subjectivity, not purely factual matters. Second, too much disagreement occurs in moral judgments for us to suppose they reflect something objective. "It makes sense to accept our observations of physical objects as legitimate partly because we all agree on them. . .the intersubjective agreement necessary to legitimate moral observations is not present."[14] Third, we don't perceive moral features or values, though we should if they were objective properties of our world. Thus, Gilbert Harman notes:

> Can moral principles be tested. . .out in the world? You can observe someone do something, but can you ever perceive the

> rightness or wrongness of what he does? If you round a corner and see a group of young hoodlums pour gasoline on a cat and ignite it, you do not need to *conclude* that what they are doing is wrong; you do not need to figure anything out; you can *see* that it is wrong. But is your reaction due to the actual wrongness of what you see or is it simply a reflection of your moral "sense," a "sense" that you have acquired perhaps as a result of your moral upbringing?[15]

The first reason for moral "skepticism" is weak. It is question–begging to insist that what is objective and descriptive is value-neutral, or that it is inappropriate for us to react emotionally to it. If there are value-facts about the world, it is precisely these we should respond to "with an attitude." In a similar way, if there are fearful or painful things in the world, it is certainly appropriate for us to respond to these with fear or pain. If there are colorful things in our world, we should respond to these by recognizing their colors. Why should we assume that facts or objective concepts must be free of value or that they should fail to provoke our emotions? This is a built-in bias, and an argument needs to be given why objective facts must be eunuchs. Otherwise, it is quite possible that some objective facts are value-laden while others are not. True, our emotions can obscure our judgment so that we ignore relevant facts, but this does not mean that all emotional responses are definitive of non-objective judgment. It is inappropriate to become fearful at the prospect that the house has a red roof or that $6 + 4 = 10$, but wholly appropriate to do so when told "We will torture you." Why not view the negative emotional responses and negative value-connotations of injustice, murder, theft, and adultery in the same way? The fact that we initially learn these negative associations by teaching and conditioning does not show these evaluations are without objective foundation. No more can we show that most of what we learn is merely the product of social conditioning simply because we accept as trustworthy the claims made by textbooks or authority-figures.

Next consider skepticism based on the lack of agreement in moral judgments. This objection rests on a dubious view of the relationship between facts and human reality. The suggestion is that if something is an objective feature of reality and a feature with which we are familiar, either it will overwhelm us with its objective status, or it will be so neutral or unambiguous that no bias or emotion on our part will prevent us from recognizing its objective status. In such a vast and intricate cosmos, which includes the complex motivational structure of human beings, why in the world should we accept such a presumption? Just as plausible is the presumption that objective fact is weak and underwhelming in its appeal to most of us.

Many reasons exist why we can fail to acknowledge fact or fail to agree about what the facts are, reasons which have nothing to do with whether the "facts" are subjective or objective.[16] Consider the following factors which can hamper, distort, or block human judgment and consensus.

(1) Powerful emotions (which need not express themselves in powerful or exaggerated overt behavior): anger, vengeance, hatred, love, fear, envy, greed, vanity, etc.
(2) Limitations on the information available to us (externally imposed or self-imposed, censorship or wishful thinking)
(3) The complexity, vagueness, or ambiguity of the world, and ourselves. For example, no sharp boundary exists between a mountain and a hill, a child and an adult, day-night-twilight, one shade of color and another color.
(4) Political, cultural, or religious ideology, and the pressures, some subtle and others gross, to conform to religious or secular icons
(5) Habit and our desire for order, security, and continuity
(6) Our desire for simplicity and our tendency to oversimplify
(7) Our ability to rationalize in order to preserve our "idealized" image of ourselves and what we care for

We are not recording machines but emotional beings with insecurities and fallibilities, creatures whose subjective nature can easily cloud our judgment. The ability to be an objective, impartial, and careful observer is largely learned and is not easy. Contrary to providing a careful (and personally non-threatening) description of the colors, textures, weight, etc. of some object, moral descriptions involve complications of personal responsibility, blame, punishment, damage to our self-image, psychological defense mechanisms, and powerful emotions. Such factors make it unreasonable to expect that if a definite right and wrong exists, we will agree about what they are.[17]

These same considerations apply to moral disagreements between societies. Each society has an intricate system of value-standards which includes a structure of value-priorities. Even if some set of universally applicable moral standards exists, our human fallibilism could easily prevent a society's practices from conforming to it. Just as individuals can lose touch with what is most important, so too can societies misplace their priorities. Socrates considered his role to be a gadfly, to make sure the Athenians did not fall into corrupt ways due to laziness or lack of alertness. If societies can betray their own ideals, we should not be surprised that they can differ with one another over what is right.

Finally, consider the objection that we do not perceive moral values or properties. We can perceive lies, thefts, adultery, murder, etc., but we do not perceive what makes them wrong. Thus, moral properties are not discovered, but projected or superimposed by individual or cultural perspectives. In other words, moral standards are either subjective or culturally relative.

Before addressing this objection head-on, notice that it can equally well be launched against any set of values. There are far-reaching consequences of accepting this point of view. Moral values are only a species of value. There are scientific, mathematical, logical, and practical values. Ethical subjectivism itself embodies a value. Subjectivists suppose that their view is superior to the objectivist view, presumably because they imagine that their view is true whereas objectivism is nonfactual and illusory. For subjectivists, ethical subjectivism *is* a value-standard. The problem is that we no more (empirically) perceive what makes subjectivism "good" than we perceive what makes justice morally good. Put another way, the same grounds for holding the worth of moral value to be imperceivable are also grounds for holding the worth of subjectivism to be imperceivable. If the subjectivist argues that we perceive the preferability of subjectivism by considering that it conforms to fact, is consistent, or meets some other value-standard, this will be an appeal to a value whose desirability is no more open to public perception than is moral goodness. For example, suppose the subjectivist argues that following subjectivism contributes to our survival (an unlikely result in any event). We will have to point out that although we can perceive why people do or do not survive, we do not perceive–on subjectivist perceptual grounds–what is good about survival. This subjectivist argument is not only devastating for ethical subjectivism, but also for science, mathematics, logic, and common sense. But if the same argument which undermines your opponent's view also undermines your view, you ought to reconsider the argument. Otherwise, you would be committed to throwing out the baby with the bath water. I am addressing here only those who feel moral values and are wholly subjective while believing that other values are objective. I know of no way to prove the more sweeping subjectivism to be "false." I'm not sure I even understand what such subjectivists mean by "true" and "false."[5]

Such are the generalized implications of moral subjectivism when based on the argument that we do not perceive moral value. The moral relativist (based on cultural differences) may argue for this perspective based on what we do perceive about moral value standards. Here the argument is not that justice, for example, is subjective and invented, but that the objectivity of "justice" is wholly relative to the customs of our culture. According to this argument from perception, since we fail to perceive moral standards which are constant and universal, we have no reason to believe in moral absolutes. We do perceive (using a broad notion of perceive) moral standards, but no moral Standard. The moral standard in our culture may be individual and corporate freedom, while in other cultures, contrary standards may serve as moral beacons.

The absolutist will want to reply to this that the argument is beside the point, since it fails to distinguish between the standard of right and wrong versus accepted, applied, or misapplied standards of right and wrong. Suppose, for example, that the absolute standard of moral right is whatever promotes the least injury to all involved. This standard will remain invariant, even if it is perceived in its application (or misapplication) to vary from one culture's commitment to private enterprise, to another culture's commitment to public ownership, or to a hybrid of these two.

By the same token, you can no more refute the existence of variety by employing Parmenides' standards of "pure" logic and metaphysics. Using Parmenides' logic, you can equally well argue that variation is only an illusion of our perception, since variation implies a constant which varies over time, a constant which is not identical with perceived variation, hence something which is invariant. Pursuing this ancient logic, since it is the invariant which seems to vary according to our perception and since the invariant (by definition) cannot vary–all perceived variation must be illusory.

Neither can you avoid this conclusion by arguing that variation does not presuppose anything which remains the same throughout the apparent variation. Another philosopher, Heraclitus, argued that everything in the world is constantly changing, hence we can never step twice into the same water in a river. As an ironic disciple of Heraclitus is supposed to have remarked, "If everything is flux, then one cannot even step into the *same* water *once*."[18] In other words, if pressed to its logical conclusion, a radical denial of any stable constants implies that you cannot even think of "the" process of change (flux) as a single or coherent process. If everything is continually changing, then this will be true not only from moment to moment, but also within any moment. Each "moment" of time would be continually changing so that no moment will be identical with itself. No "moment" will endure long enough to be itself. Thus, the customs of our culture will not persist long enough to be specified, or to serve as the identifiable basis for moral judgments. This abstract point I offer to show the absurdity of a particular relativist maneuver, not because I endorse Parmenidean metaphysics.

Another way exists to demonstrate the inadequacy of this relativist argument from perception. Suppose we ask whether a single relativist standard of ethical value exists, or merely a variety of ethical relativisms, including individual relativism (subjectivism) and cultural relativism. If relativists deny this, they not only will have to deny the evidence of perception, but they will open the door for the absolutist to reply that in the same way a distinction exists between invariant moral Value and varying interpretations of that Value.

Let us assume, therefore, that the ethical relativist replies (in the most natural way) that only different theories of ethical relativism exist. Notice, however, that individual relativism implies that cultural relativism is false, while cultural relativism implies likewise that individual relativism's way of fixing moral value is in error. It's not that we can't conceive of a situation where all the individuals of a culture happened to concur with the value traditions of the culture (though history and present times indicate this would be unusual). The point is that this equivalence of cultural customs and individuals' beliefs would be purely coincidental and tell us nothing about why the moral judgments were justified. Practically speaking, we cannot accept both of these theories, yet one seems as good as the other. At this point, advocates of relativism may object that these are merely different theories, not competing in the sense of being logical contradictories of each other. They may support this by urging that there is no common ground or value-standard, Truth, by which we can measure different ethical theories. Instead, we can only say that one ethical theory is true–for some people while another theory is true–for others.

At this point, another problem arises. If ethical theories cannot contradict one another, the same reasoning would imply that ethical relativism and ethical absolutism cannot contradict one another. Since the absolutist employs a different standard of evaluating ethical truth, it also follows–according to this version of ethical relativism–that we can be just as wise to accept ethical absolutism as we are to accept ethical relativism. We apparently could accept both simultaneously without fear of inconsistency. If the ethical relativist is willing to go this far in order to press a critique of absolutism, surely the absolutist can reply that absolutism contains nothing which is this strange. Such a view would be practically useless for us, since we demand of a world-view that it impose some restrictions on what is and what is not acceptable. This version of ethical relativism violates this practical need since it implies that we have no reason to prefer ethical relativism over its "competitor," ethical absolutism. To summarize this discussion, the argument from perception seems to fail because it equally undermines ethical relativism.

In conclusion, I urge that nothing is especially problematic about the nature of moral value in comparison to other values. Whatever grounds for skepticism which can be urged to beset the objectivity or constancy of moral value standards will also be found to beset the alleged objectivity or constancy of any value standard. For example, on a suitably narrow and traditional model of perception, it is just as difficult to observe scientific or mathematical values as it is to see moral values "in the world." How could we observe what makes the repeatability of experiments valuable? How could we observe the value of logical consistency? Perhaps radical skepticism is the best attitude to adopt about all truth (though it is not for me). I have not tried to refute such skepticism, but only to suggest that if we are willing to accept any objective or constant value-standards, we should be equally willing to accept the existence of such standards for moral judgments.[19]

Having considered standard arguments against the objectivity or constancy of moral value standards, it is now time to say in what sense I hold that such standards are objective. Do I mean to say that moral right and wrong are worldly qualities which we perceive? If not, how can it be credible that justice, for example, is known to us in an objective fashion?

In saying that moral standards like honesty, compassion, fairness, and justice are "objective," I mean that their worth is independent of anyone's belief to the contrary. Fortunately, it is hard to find many people now, or at any time in the past, who are prepared sincerely to make such a contrary judgment. The constancy of the global consensus of attitudes toward these values is like (though not as widely shared as) our consensus toward the independent status of physical objects. We believe that physical objects exist independently of our attitudes and perceptions, and our belief remains firm even in the face of the skeptical argument that we are unable to prove that such objects exist, at least by appeal to perception. "I am aware that skepticism about the external world is widely thought to have been refuted, but I have remained convinced of its irrefutability since being exposed at Berkeley to Thomas Clark's largely unpublished ideas on the subject."[20] As the philosopher Berkeley pointed out,[21] everything we know about chairs, trees, and other physical objects (except their existence even when no one is perceiving them) is dependent on our perceptual experience. We are never able to perceive things when we are not perceiving them. Since everything we can confirm (or refute) about physical things (including our bodies) is possible only through our perception: (1) we have extremely strong probabilistic evidence that physical objects are dependent upon our perception for their existence, and (2) the possibility remains that no object exists outside of the sphere of consciousness. Thus, Berkeley concluded that the very nature of "physical objects" lies in their being perceived by someone (if only by God).

I would not go this far, and I do not mean to advocate skepticism about the existence of physical objects. Berkeley's argument does not prove the non-existence of independent physical objects, but only that we cannot prove their existence on the basis of perception. I would, therefore, draw a different conclusion, reminding you that physical objects are considered by us the very paradigms of objective existence. If such independent objects exist, and if we know they exist (both of which I believe), then we are helpless to justify these convictions by appealing to what we perceive. But no philosopher or skeptic has shown (to my knowledge) that we *need* to be able to justify these convictions.

Odd as it may seem, these reflections are relevant to whether moral value standards are objective and whether we perceive the wrongness, say, of cruelty. Let us suppose that independent objects like physical objects exist, and we are aware of their existence through our perception, yet we cannot prove either of these propositions by appeal to our perception. If physical reality (and I include molecules, atoms and quarks here) can exist in this manner, then we have no reason why moral reality cannot exist in a similar way. In other words, moral value-standards like honesty, compassion, fairness, and justice may have objective worth, and we may be aware of this through perception, yet we may be unable to prove this by appeal to perception. Let me state the point in a more negative way, though in a more powerful form. If we cannot prove the objective existence of physical objects–a paradigm of objectivity–on the basis of perception, yet we feel entitled to believe that they do exist, it is intellectually unfair to insist that the objectivity of moral values is dubious because we cannot justify this by appeal to perception. If we think the objectivity of moral values is refuted by the evidence of perception, we ought also to abandon our faith in the objective status of physical objects.

The preceding has been a tedious way of arguing that the reasonableness of holding that moral value-standards are objective cannot be wed to whether we can prove this on the basis of perception. A corollary of this conclusion is that moral value-standards may be objective even if we do not perceive them. Plato argued for this, and even if his theory of the forms is unacceptable, he may have been correct in thinking that much (he said all) of our knowledge is not derived from our five senses, but from our intelligence and reason. Let me sketch one possible account of how this might work. Suppose our brain gives us more than the ability to synthesize, analyze, and classify the information we receive by means of our bodily senses. Suppose it also gives us the ability to apprehend (like our sight gives us colors, shapes, etc.) "facts." One of these facts might be that physical objects exist–objects which exist independently of our perceptions and beliefs, and which manifest themselves through the sensations we have of seeing, touching, hearing, etc. Another of these facts might be that justice is independently worthwhile, no matter how it is manifested to individual perspectives, given the limitations of experience, upbringing and reasoning. I don't claim this is the way our brain works, but I do claim it is conceivable that much of our knowledge is gained in this way.

I am far more confident of the objectivity and constancy of moral value-standards like justice and compassion than I am about how we come by this knowledge. I don't know if we perceive what is right about justice in the sense that we discover this through perceiving the world of just and unjust actions, laws, institutions, etc. Here is another way of accounting for the objectivity and constancy of moral value-standards. Kant suggested that, we human beings have our own species-relative way of conceptualizing the world of our perceptions.[22] One way of understanding Kant's view is to imagine that between ourselves and the world are two filters, one of perception and the other of conceptualization. Through perception, we are acquainted with phenomena as they are situated in time and space (space and time never appearing to us as objects). Through the kinds of concepts and categories we have as human beings, the phenomena of our sense-perception are ordered and classified. Thus, we understand what we perceive as singular or diverse, even or odd, human or non-human, above or below, and all particular occurrences are understood by us to be the effects of causes.

Our filters delimit for us the world we can understand, but this does not mean our way of understanding is the only way the world can be perceived or conceptualized. Bats, for example, perceive phenomena (as part of their natural sonar, navigational system) which we human beings do not. Furthermore, intelligent creatures may exist who conceptualize the world differently than we do–say, Martians who are unable to have the concept of games or who have concepts to which we are hopelessly blind. Viewed in this way, the way we perceive and conceive is not necessarily the way other species perceive and conceive–but a great deal of our perceptual and conceptual scheme is universal among human beings. Thus, people in other cultures may not perceive the same sorts of trees and plants as do we, but we all share the concept of trees and plants, and see the colors of plants according to a shared spectrum of colors. In other words, the particulars we perceive will vary according to time and place, but the form of our perception and concepts will overlap. The standard for correctly identifying and applying the perceptual or conceptual scheme of a species (as Aristotle long ago argued) is not the exception but the rule–the way human beings for the most part perceive or conceive. Thus, we are not prepared to revise our understanding of color, or its objectivity, simply because a few humans are blind or because some are color-blind to some colors in some contexts. Universal access or openness to a phenomenon or quality is not considered essential to our assessment that it is objective or that there are (*homo sapiens*-relative) appropriate ways of identifying it. For example, it is not appropriate to judge the color of an object while bathed in a red light, but only in sunlight or (if indoors or at night) under uniform, white artificial light.

We can apply this Kantian view to moral concepts. When it comes to understanding and categorizing actions, rules, laws, policies, institutions, people, etc., part of our conceptual scheme may be that we conceptualize in terms of concepts like justice and fairness. Other forms of life (Martians and dogs), may lack moral concepts. If so, we cannot reasonably expect their attitudes and behavior to be restrained by such normative ideals.

Justice conceived in this Kantian way would validate to some degree Protagoras' ancient claim than "Man is the measure of all things." Moral value-standards would have objective validity, but only within the human family or within species that possessed the concept of justice. For members of other species not possessing this concept, judgments about justice would be quite empty and meaningless. If this is the best way to interpret the scope of our moral judgments, then the moral community of discourse is sufficiently extensive (covering the human species) to bridge individual preferences and cultural differences among human beings. Indeed, we could say that the most inclusive world culture is defined by the basic moral norms of justice, compassion, and health–norms of the human family. Thus, human culture would bridge the provincialism of nationality, race, and ethnicity.

13. Why Should We Act Morally?

Philosophers and other thinkers have long wondered whether we have any good reason for acting morally. What is good about justice, health, and compassion? Will we personally benefit from acting justly, or is it a simple-minded foolishness, an irksome necessary evil at best?

These issues were addressed long ago by Plato in his *Republic*, and his general answer still is correct. He argued that justice was intrinsically worthwhile and also worthwhile for the advantages it produces for our social well-being. Beginning with the intrinsic worth of acting justly, being healthy, and being compassionate, I would say that each of these is admirable even when they do not lead a person to happiness. Given our finite limitations and our inherent vulnerability to factors beyond our control, no attitude or action can guarantee that we will avoid pain or unhappiness. Whether we act justly or unjustly, more powerful forces in society or nature may still cause us great misfortune.

Many people may find the notion of intrinsic goods or evils to be dubious, so I will not argue for the intrinsic worth of justice. The real issue lies elsewhere. The question has always been: Which is more advantageous to us, acting justly or acting unjustly? Since there are no absolute guarantees of what will follow our actions, we should evaluate this issue in terms of which is more likely to promote human well-being. Guided by the norm of healthy self-development, we are more likely to be happy if we treat ourselves with care and respect. The many forms of self-neglect and abuse bring us misery.

Are we more likely to benefit if we treat others with justice and compassion? If God exists and is just, we can expect divine rewards of some sort, but we can hardly rest this issue in the hands of religious faith. If all of us, or most of us, treated each other with compassion and justice, significant benefit would come to everyone. Conversely, if all of us, or most of us, acted unjustly and heartlessly, significant harm would be done to us. The trade-off from accepting and "enforcing" a moral code which reveres justice is that we gain dependability and security in human interactions at the cost of some personal freedom and pleasure.

Some ethical theorists see the personal advantages to be gained if everyone behaved justly, but they are reasonably skeptical that any such perfection can be achieved in human affairs. "What if I behave justly while others treat me unjustly?" Here lies the source of doubt about whether we are better off acting morally than immorally. It certainly can happen that our just behavior profits us little when others are unjustly taking advantage of our good nature. How likely is it that many more people will act justly rather than unjustly toward their neighbors? The probabilities depend on more than how people behave. They also depend on how we perceive each other's behavior (whether as just or unjust) and how we subjectively estimate that people will behave in the future.

I doubt that any precise and definitive answer can be given about how likely it is that a substantial majority of people will behave justly at any given time. Nevertheless, the reply suggested by Plato in the *Republic* still serves as a most reasonable conjecture. Almost all of us come to realize that we are not strong enough, cunning enough, or intelligent enough to get away with doing injustice to others. Life continues to make clear to us in a vast number of ways how vulnerable we are. Our injustices are detected and other people retaliate. Other times, we punish ourselves for our perceived wrongs by the sting of our guilty conscience. Our experience and most of literature throughout human history makes evident that most of us do not think we are capable of achieving the happiness gained by powerfully unjust people. Furthermore, we greatly desire to avoid having injustice done to us. We also realize that our only realistic protection against suffering injustice is to encourage the institutions of self-restraint necessary to reinforce just behavior and punish unjust behavior. Therefore, most people will likely prefer to honor justice over injustice. This does not mean they will always act justly, but only that they will accept the norm of justice as the legitimate standard of how we should behave. Thus, they will teach their children self-restraint through telling the truth, not stealing, keeping their word, etc. They will try to act justly, and will support the need for law and order, and a criminal justice system that treats the rich and the poor offender equally. This means that most of us will benefit from such self-restraint, but a few powerful people will also benefit by acting unjustly (as wolves among a flock of sheep). Regrettable as this injustice is, it still shows ironically that all of us–both the just and the unjust– stand to gain from the socialized practice of justice.

What about the wolves among the sheep? If acting justly is in the self-interest of the sheep, would it also be so for the wolves? Would they gain even more (or lose less) if they behaved justly? Plato argued they too would be better off if they changed their corrupt ways to those of justice.[23] I am not sure of this, but there are serious disadvantages to the life of those who are unjust and powerful. For example, if you want power and want to preserve it, you need to protect yourself from getting caught and punished for your acts of injustice. It is not easy to preserve great power. You have to invest much time and energy to do so. Keeping your deception undercover is in itself a task that requires continuing strenuous effort. It is hard to trust others, especially those closest to you. They may try to usurp your power. True or lasting friends are hard to come by. Such a life can be lonely. The greater your injustices, the more you may fear severe punishment should you be found out and held accountable. The more your injustices are known, the more anger and hatred will be directed toward you. So, if the rewards of great injustice are extreme, so too are the penalties for the fall. Consider the frequent fates of deposed dictators. They are often forced into permanent exile, ridiculed and harassed in their exile, obliged to look over their shoulder for the feared assassin, and even assassinated. The latter days of the Shah of Iran, Somoza of Nicaragua, or Ferdinand Marcos of the Philippines are hardly to be envied by anyone.

As unhappy and tormented as the lives of the unjust can be, I don't think this is decisive. Extreme misery can befall any of us, whether just or unjust, and it may be that for some types of personalities (fortunately few in number), the intense rewards counterbalance the intense costs of such extreme living. We should think not of the addictive gambler who seldom wins, but of the rare gambler who is successful much of the time. Perhaps such people would be far unhappier if they were forced to greatly restrain themselves and lead a generally just life. Perhaps they would be as happy or happier. Our temperaments can change significantly as our habits change. After we work our way through a painful change in lifestyle, we can decide that the new habits are more rewarding than the abandoned ones. As it happens, those who lead the lives of great extremes, including great injustice, typically fall rapidly and far when their fortunes shift. For this reason, neither they nor we have the opportunity to judge whether a more ordinary and restrained lifestyle would have pleased them as much as their life of extremes.

In conclusion, I have not sought to prove that a general commitment to living morally will be personally advantageous to all of us. I have presented reasons for thinking that such a general commitment will be advantageous to the great majority of human beings. Indeed, the commitment of societies to justice has the ironic advantage of promoting the self-interest of the just and the unjust alike. If my reasoning has been sound, we can be confident that immense value is to be gained overall if we act justly. If most of us managed to act perfectly justly, we might succeed at uncovering and then disempowering those who are unjust. This would not be advantageous to the interests of the extremely unjust. Still, if they really endorse the view that justice is the interests of the "stronger," then they should concede that we (who would then be the stronger) had treated them justly.

NOTES

PREFACE

1. Christopher Lasch, *The Culture of Narcissism* (New York: Warner Books, 1979).

2. Karen Horney, *Neurosis and Human Growth*, ch. 8, (New York and London: W. W. Norton and Company, 1950).

3. Richard Bach, *Illusions: The Adventures of a Reluctant Messiah* (New York: Delacorte Press, 1978).

4. Plato, *Republic*, V 479-480. Aristotle, *Nicomachean Ethics* 1139a - 1142b.

CHAPTER THREE

1. Plato, *Republic*.

2. Friedrich Nietzsche, *The Will to Power* (New York: Vintage Books, 1968), and *The Genealogy of Morals* (New York: Vintage Books, 1967), ed. Walter Kaufmann.

3. Roger Ringer, *Looking Out for Number One* (New York: Fawcett Crest Book, 1989).

4. Harry Browne, *How I Found Freedom in an Unfree World* (New York: Macmillan, 1973).

5. Ayn Rand, *The Virtue of Selfishness* (New York: Signet Books, 1964).

6. Edward Regis, Jr., "What Is Ethical Egoism?", *Ethics,* 91 (1980).

7. Ringer, *Looking Out, p. 21. "So-called self-sacrifice is just an irrationally selfish act (doing what you think will make you feel good) . . . "*

8. *Ibid.,* p. 10. "Because people always do that which they *think* will bring them the greatest pleasure, selfishness is not the issue."

9. Gospel of Matthew, 22: 36-40, and Gospel of Luke, 10: 25-28.

10. B. F. Skinner, *Beyond Freedom and Dignity* (New York: Bantam/Vintage, 1971). See his chapter on "Freedom."

11. Plato, *Protagoras*, 358; Jean-Paul Sartre, "Existentialism Is a Humanism," *Existentialism,* ed. Robert Solomon (New York: The Modern Library, 1974), pp. 198-199.

12. For a similar view of self-concern versus selfishness, see Eric Fromm, *The Art of Loving* (New York: Harper and Row, 1989), pp. 53-55.

13. George Orwell, *1984* (New York: The New American Library, 1981).

CHAPTER FOUR

1. See Plato's *Republic*, X, 613-620. Also see Aristotle's *Nicomachean Ethics*, III, 1110a -1115a.
2. Augustine, *City of God*, V, pp. 9-10.
3. What I have offered here is only a bare-bones synopsis of what I consider to be the essential debate over our freedom and responsibility. Philosophers have continued to debate this issue in increasingly subtle and sophisticated terms. For the reader who desires a more in-depth sampling of these developments, I recommend *Determinism and Freedom in the Age of Modern Science*, ed. Sidney Hook (London: Collier Books, 1961). *Free Will and Determinism*, ed. Bernard Berofsky (New York and London: Harper and Row, 1966). Peter Van Inwagen, *An Essay On Free Will* (Oxford: Clarendon Press, 1983). Richard Double, *The Non-Reality of Free Will* (New York: Oxford University Press, 1991).
4. For a similar view, see Double, *ibid.*, ch. 5.
5. Immanuel Kant, *Critique of Pure Reason* (1781).
6. See Leibniz's *Discourse on Metaphysics*, XIII, (La Salle, Ill.: Open Court, 1968), pp. 19-23.
7. David Hume, *Treatise of Human Nature* (Oxford: Clarendon Press, Book I, 1967), Pt. III, XIV, pp. 165-166: "This therefore is the essence of necessity. Upon the whole, necessity is something that exists in the mind not in objects; nor is it possible for us ever to form the most distant idea of it, considered as a quality in bodies."
8. Carl Hempel, "The Function of General Laws in History," *Journal of Philosophy*, 39 (1942).
9. Van Inwagen, *An Essay*, pp. 138-140.
10. Debra Rosen, "A Probabilistic Theory of Causal Necessity," *The Southern Journal of Philosophy*, 18 (1980).
11. Ted Honderich, *Mind and Brain: A Theory of Determinism* (New York: Oxford University Press, 1988), p. 202.
12. *Ibid.*, pp. 68-69.
13. *Ibid.*, p. 202.
14. For more on the contexual nature of human action explanations, see my "An Alternative to Aune's Idealized View of Practi-

cal Reasoning," *The Southern Journal of Philosophy,* 18 (1980), pp. 31-36.

15. Honderich, *Mind*, p. 69.

16. Aristotle, *Metaphysics*, Book I 983b, Book V 1013a.

17. David Hume, *An Enquiry Concerning Human Understanding* (Indianapolis: Hackett, 1977), p. 51.

18. Van Inwagen, *An Essay*, p. 198.

19. William James, *Essays in Pragmatism*, ed. Alburey Castell (New York and London: Hafner Publishing, 1966), p. 142.

20. Willard Quine and J.S. Ullian, *The Web of Belief* (New York: Random House, 1970), p. 68.

21. Willard Quine, "Two Dogmas of Empiricism," *From a Logical Point of View* (New York: Harper and Row, 1961), pp. 41-43.

CHAPTER FIVE

1. Gospel of Matthew, 22: 36-40. Gospel of Mark, 12: 28-31.

2. Jeremy Bentham, *The Principles of Morals and Legislation* (1789). John Stuart Mill, *Utilitarianism* (1863).

3. John Locke, *The Second Treatise of Government*, 1690. Jean-Jacques Rousseau, *The Social Contract* (1762).

4. Speaking of the basis for civilized society, Rousseau says, ". . .instead of destroying natural equality, the fundamental pact, on the contrary, substitutes a moral and lawful equality for the physical inequality which nature imposed upon men, so that, although unequal in strength or intellect, they all become equal by convention and legal right." "The Social Contract," *Rousseau,* ed. Maurice Cranston (New York: Macmillan, 1988), p. 129.

5. See, for example, Thomas Aquinas, *Summa Theologica*.

6. Aristotle, *Nicomachean Ethics*, Book II.

7. Immanuel Kant, *Fundamental Principles of The Metaphysics of Morals* (1785).

8. The most recent and sophisticated account of justice is John Rawls, *A Theory of Justice* (Cambridge, Mass.: Harvard University Press, 1971).

9. Plato advances a similar argument in the *Republic*, Book I, 334-335, and in the *Crito*, 48e-50a.

10. Plato, *Crito*.

11. G.E. Moore, *Principia Ethica* (1903).

12. David Hume, *A Treatise of Human Nature*, Book III (Oxford: Clarendon Press, 1967).

13. John Searle, “Deriving ‘Ought’ from ‘Is’,” *Speech Acts,* (Cambridge, Mass.: The University Press, 1969).

14. B.C. Postow, “Werner’s Ethical Realism,” *Ethics,* 95, (October 1984-July 1985), p. 288.

15. Gilbert Harman, *The Nature of Morality* (Oxford: Oxford University Press, 1977), p. 4.

16. See William Wainwright, “Does Disagreement Imply Relativism?”, *International Philosophical Quarterly,* 26 (1986). He also argues that the link between agreement and objective truth is dubious.

17. See Richard Werner, “Ethical Realism Defended,” *Ethics,* 95, (October 1984-July 1985). He argues that intersubjective agreement cannot be the litmus test of the objectivity of moral facts.

18. Søren Kierkegaard, *Fear and Trembling* (Garden City, N.Y.: Doubleday, 1954), p. 132.

19. I have earlier advanced these arguments in my “In Defense of Ethical Absolutism,” *Inquiries Into Values,* ed. Sander Lee (Lewiston, N.Y.: The Edwin Mellen Press, 1988). For more discussion of skepticism, see my “Kekes and Johnson on Rationality,” *The Philosophical Quarterly* (July 1978), and my “Scepticism Revisited,” *Philosophy* (July 1987).

20. Thomas Nagel, “The Absurd,” reprinted from the *Journal of Philosophy,* ed. Johnathan Westphal and Carl Levenson, *Life and Death* (Indianapolis: Hackett, 1993), p. 93. Also see section five of the same article.

21. George Berkeley, *A Treatise Concerning The Principles of Human Knowledge* (1734).

22. Kant, *The Critique of Pure Reason* (1781).

23. Plato, *Republic*, VIII 562-IX 579. He also offers a religious rationale for this contention in the *Republic*, X 613e-620. This “day of judgment” rationale also occurs in Plato’s *Gorgias*, and *Phaedo.*

BIBLIOGRAPHY

Aquinas, Thomas. *Summa Theologica.*

Aristotle. *De Anima.*

Aristotle. *Nicomachean Ethics.*

Augustine. *The City of God.*

Bach, Richard. *Illusions: The Adventures of a Reluctant Messiah.* New York: Delacorte, 1978.

Bentham, Jeremy. *The Principles of Morals and Legislation.*

Berkeley, George. *A Treatise Concerning The Principles of Human Knowledge.* 1734.

Berofsky, Bernard. *Free Will and Determinism.* New York and London: Harper and Row, 1966.

Browne, Harry. *How I Found Freedom in an Unfree World.* New York: Macmillan, 1973.

Double, Richard. *The Non-Reality of Free Will.* New York: Oxford University Press, 1991.

Fowler, Corbin. "An Alternative to Aune's Idealized View of Practical Reasoning," *The Southern Journal of Philosophy*, 9, 1980.

_____. "In Defense of Ethical Absolutism," *Inquiries into Values.* Ed. Sander Lee. Lewiston, N.Y.: The Edwin Mellen Press, 1988.

______. "Kekes and Johnson on Rationality," *The Philosophical Quarterly.* July, 1978.

_____. "Skepticism Revisited," *Philosophy*, July 1987.

Fromm, Eric. *The Art of Loving.* New York: Harper and Row, 1989.

Harman, Gilbert. *The Nature of Morality.* Oxford: Oxford University Press, 1977.

Honderich, Ted. *Mind and Brain: A Theory of Determinism.* New York: Oxford University Press, 1988.

Hook, Sidney. *Determinism and Freedom in the Age of Modern Sciences.* London: Collier Books, 1961.

Horney, Karen. *Neurosis and Human Growth.* New York, London: W. W. Norton and Company, 1950.

Hume, David. *An Enquiry Concerning Human Understanding.* Indianapolis: Hackett, 1977.

______. *A Treatise of Human Nature.* Oxford: Clarendon Press, 1967.

James, William. *Essays in Pragmatism.* ed. Alburey Castell, New York, London: Hafner Publishing, 1966.

Kant, Immanuel. *The Critique of Pure Reason.* 1781.

______. *The Foundations of the Metaphysics of Morals.* 1785.

Kierkegaard, Søren. *Fear and Trembling.* Garden City, N.Y.: Anchor Books, 1954.

Lasch, Christopher. *The Culture of Narcissism.* New York: Warner Books, 1979.

Leibniz. *Discourse on Metaphysics.* LaSalle, Ill.: Open Court, 1968.

Locke, John. *The Second Treatise of Government.* 1690.

Mill, John Stuart. *Utilitarianism.* 1863.

Moore, G.E. *Principia Ethica.* 1903.

Nietzsche, Friedrich. *The Will to Power.* New York: Vintage Books, 1986.

Postow, B. C. "Werner's Ethical Realism," *Ethics*, 95, October 1984 - July 1985.

Plato. *Crito.*

______. *Euthyphro.*

______. *Gorgias.*

______. *Phaedo.*

______. *Republic.*

Quine, W. V. O. *From a Logical Point of View.* New York: Harper and Row, 1961.

Quine, W. V. O., and J. S. Ullian. *The Web of Belief.* New York: Random House, 1970.

Rand, Ayn. *The Virtue of Selfishness.* New York: Signet Books, 1964.

Rawls, John. *A Theory of Justice.* Cambridge, Mass.: Harvard University Press, 1971.

Regis, Edward Jr. "What is Ethical Egoism?", *Ethics*, 91, 1980.

Ringer, Roger. *Looking Out For Number One.* New York: Fawcett Crest Book, 1989.

Rosen, Debra. "A Probabilistic Theory of Causal Necessity," *The Southern Journal of Philosophy*, 18, 1980.

Rousseau, Jean-Jacques. *The Social Contract.* 1762.

Searle, John. *Speech Acts.* Cambridge, Mass.: The University Press, 1969.

Solomon, Robert. *Existentialism.* New York: The Modern Library, 1974.

Van Inwagen, Peter. *An Essay on Free Will.* Oxford: Clarendon Press, 1983.

Wainwright, William. "Does Disagreement Imply Relativism?", *International Philosophical Quarterly*, 26, 1986.

Werner, Richard. "Ethical Realism Defended," *Ethics*, 95, October 1984 - July 1985.

ABOUT THE AUTHOR

Dr. Fowler is the author of a critique of U.S. strategic policy: *The Logic of U.S. Nuclear Weapons Policy* (1987). He has also published articles in various professional journals, including *The Philosophical Quarterly*, *Philosophy*, and *The Southern Journal of Philosophy*. The topics of his journal publications include animals' right to freedom, the question of mind-body identity, knowledge and skepticism, U.S. nuclear weapons policy, theory of action, and ethical theory. Dr. Fowler has delivered numerous presentations at professional conferences in Europe as well as in the United States. He is a member of the American and International Societies for Value Inquiry, and he is the current Secretary of the Association of Philosophy and Religious Studies of the Pennsylvania State System of Higher Education. Since the late 1960s, he has been an activist for peace and justice on campus and in the community. Currently, Dr. Fowler is Assistant Professor of Philosophy at Edinboro University of Pennsylvania.

INDEX

VIBS

1. Noel Balzer, **The Human Being as a Logical Thinker**.
2. Archie J. Bahm, **Axiology: The Science of Values.**
3. H. P. P. (Hennie) Lötter, **Justice for an Unjust Society.**
4. H. G. Callaway, **Context for Meaning and Analysis: A Critical Study in the Philosophy of Language.**
5. Benjamin S. Llamzon, **A Humane Case for Moral Intuition.**
6. James R. Watson, **Between Auschwitz and Tradition: Postmodern Reflections on the Task of Thinking.** A volume in **Holocaust and Genocide Studies.**
7. Robert S. Hartman, **Freedom to Live: The Robert Hartman Story,** edited by Arthur R. Ellis. A volume in **Hartman Institute Axiology Studies.**
8. Archie J. Bahm, **Ethics: The Science of Oughtness.**
9. George David Miller: **An Idiosyncratic Ethics; Or, the Lauramachean Ethics.**
10. Joseph P. DeMarco, **A Coherence Theory in Ethics.**

11. Frank G. Forrest, **Valuemetrics$^{\aleph}$: The Science of Personal and Professional Ethics.** A volume in **Hartman Institute Axiology Studies.**

12. William Gerber, **The Meaning of Life: Insights of the World's Great Thinkers.**

13. Richard T. Hull, Editor, **A Quarter Century of Value Inquiry: Presidential Addresses of the American Society for Value Inquiry.** A volume in **Histories and Addresses of Philosophical Societies.**

14. William Gerber, **Nuggets of Wisdom from Great Jewish Thinkers: From Biblical Times to the Present.**

15. Sidney Axinn, **The Logic of Hope: Extensions of Kant's View of Religion.**

16. Messay Kebede, **Meaning and Development.**

17. Amihud Gilead, **The Platonic Odyssey: A Philosophical-Literary Inquiry into the *Phaedo*.**

18. Necip Fikri Alican, **Mill's Principle of Utility: A Defense of John Stuart Mill's Notorious Proof.** A volume in **Universal Justice.**

19. Michael H. Mitias, Editor, **Philosophy and Architecture.**

20. Roger T. Simonds, **Rational Individualism: The Perennial Philosophy of Legal Interpretation.** A volume in **Natural Law Studies.**

21. William Pencak, **The Conflict of Law and Justice in the Icelandic Sagas.**

22. Samuel M. Natale and Brian M. Rothschild, Editors, **Values, Work, Education: The Meanings of Work.**

23. N. Georgopoulos and Michael Heim, Editors, **Being Human in the Ultimate: Studies in the Thought of John M. Anderson.**

24. Robert Wesson and Patricia A. Williams, Editors, **Evolution and Human Values.**

25. Wim J. van der Steen, **Facts, Values, and Methodology: A New Approach to Ethics.**

26. Avi Sagi and Daniel Statman, **Religion and Morality.**

27. Albert William Levi, **The High Road of Humanity: The Seven Ethical Ages of Western Man,** edited by Donald Phillip Verene and Molly Black Verene.

28. Samuel M. Natale and Brian M. Rothschild, Editors, **Work Values: Education, Organization, and Religious Concerns.**

29. Laurence F. Bove and Laura Duhan Kaplan, Editors, **From the Eye of the Storm: Regional Conflicts and the Philosophy of Peace.** A volume in **Philosophy of Peace.**

30. Robin Attfield, **Value, Obligation, and Meta-Ethics.**

31. William Gerber, **The Deepest Questions You Can Ask About God: As Answered by the World's Great Thinkers.**

32. Daniel Statman, **Moral Dilemmas.**

33. Rem B. Edwards, Editor, **Formal Axiology and Its Critics.** A volume in **Hartman Institute Axiology Studies.**

34. George David Miller and Conrad P. Pritscher, **On Education and Values: In Praise of Pariahs and Nomads.** A volume in **Philosophy of Education.**

35. Paul S. Penner, **Altruistic Behavior: An Inquiry into Motivation.**

36. Corbin Fowler, **Morality for Moderns.**